Cinema One

28 George Cukor

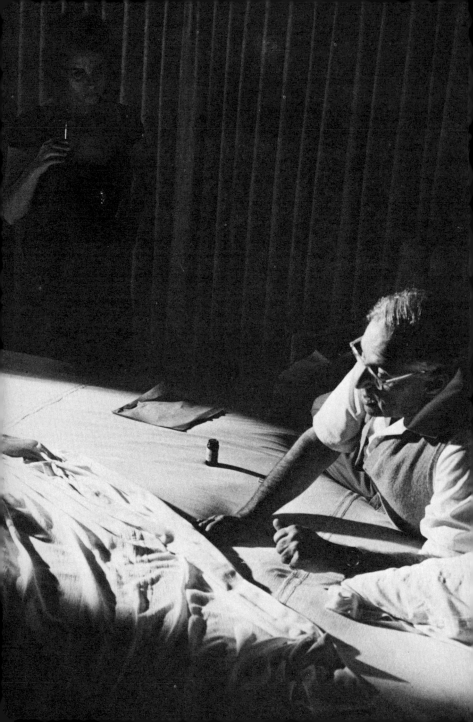

George Cukor

Carlos Clarens

London

Secker and Warburg in association with the
British Film Institute

The Cinema One Series is published by
Secker & Warburg Limited
14 Carlisle Street, Soho Square, London W1V 6NN
in association with the
British Film Institute, 81 Dean Street, London W1V 6AA

General Editors
Penelope Houston and David Wilson

George Cukor by Carlos Clarens
first published by Secker & Warburg 1976
Copyright © Carlos Clarens 1976

SBN 436 09942 X (hardcover)
SBN 436 09943 8 (paperback)

Designed by Michael Farrell

Filmset in Photon Times 11 pt by
Richard Clay (The Chaucer Press), Ltd, Bungay, Suffolk
and printed in Great Britain by
Fletcher & Son Ltd, Norwich

Contents

Introduction

Like Ford, Hawks, Leo McCarey and King Vidor, George Cukor is one of those talents which could probably only flourish within the big Hollywood factory system, thanks to (or despite) the stimulation, surveillance and interference of men like Laemmle, Mayer, Thalberg and Selznick. There is a delicate dialectic between the artistic achievement and the industrial product often and predictably established in their work, an identity imposed on intractable material despite the formidable technology of the big studios. The small personal obsessions that make up a directorial style are not necessarily cancelled out by executive interference: Hollywood art is, at its best, an art of subversion. A talent like that of von Stroheim was broken on the Hollywood wheel less because of the man's extravagance than by his artistic boasts; but, not too ironically, the same Hollywood made possible the second flowering of such foreign directors as Lubitsch, Murnau and Lang. Not that the old Hollywood did not merit its reputation; it was a system of left-handed patronage, protective and ruthless. With the exception of Chaplin, who managed to retain the autonomy of the great self-governing pioneers, the most distinguished directors in America were both victors and victims. The film career of George Cukor is strewn with incomplete, mutilated, unrealized efforts (*One Hour with You*, *Gone with the Wind*, *Desire Me*, *The Razor's Edge*, *The Chapman Report*). All the more credit to the man for consistently refusing the role of martyr to a Philistine industry, for never becoming a lost cause for critics. Like Ford, unlike Welles, Cukor instinctively realized that the limits of the Hollywood system were also its co-ordinates, and played the game accordingly.

7

In the Thirties and Forties it was simpler to regard Cukor as a superb director of actors, a craftsman of talent or, in a less sympathetic light, as a master of survival in the Hollywood scene, a transfuge from the stage, or a purveyor of escapism, rather than to grant him full admission to the circle of 'respectable' commercial directors established by Rotha, Griffith, Jacobs *et al.*, and whose members included Capra, Borzage, Wyler, Wellman, Milestone, La Cava and Kanin. Although it must be obvious that Cukor has fared infinitely better than these directors, I have no wish to displace any of them, in the manner in which nowadays Keaton is made to displace Chaplin, or Roach extolled at the expense of Sennett. Nor do I want to deplore the critical failings of another generation; every age is defined as much by its criticism as by its literature, and this should also hold true of the motion picture.

Coming of intellectual age between world wars, English-speaking critics learned to abide by an aesthetic of film dominated by social significance and the theory of montage, complementary affinities of form and content upholding socially committed criticism and evolving as much from the impact of the great Russian silents as from the inescapable realities of the Great Depression. And the Eisenstein theory of dynamic editing continued to hold up a Procrustean yardstick by which all films were critically measured until the mid-Fifties – a quarter of a century after the demise of silent films – and the arrival of Bazin and Langlois on the French scene. Until then, the ideal movie was made in the moviola, long takes were anathema, actors critical cattle and a director who renounced editing for the carefully sustained shot would be rebuked as primitive, like Chaplin, or dismissed as theatrical, like Cukor. Theatre was some kind of epithet hurled at the screen: the film, unlike the stage which has no delusions of purity, has built some formidable reservations as to what is 'cinematic' and what is not.

At least Cukor had paid his social dues once in a while, the way King Vidor did in *Our Daily Bread*, an ingratiating gesture towards the unprivileged later tarnished by *The Texas Rangers* and *Northwest Passage*. But superficially at least (for there is always *The Marrying Kind*), Cukor keeps his distance from populist causes, as much as from Westerns and gangster films, recognized Hollywood genres that travel well in critical circles. There is a telling scene in an otherwise minor Cukor comedy, *Susan and God* – in which Joan Crawford as

'Yes, *Susan*': Joan Crawford, Marjorie Main in *Susan and God*

a socialite who has suddenly discovered the brotherhood of man instructs her maid, Marjorie Main, to call her by her first name, and Ms Main complies with an ineffable, 'Yes, *Susan*' – that is worth a dozen social tracts. It seems to me to capture to perfection Cukor's attitude towards Hollywood's social conscience. It must have been obvious for someone coming from the theatre that all comedy *is* social, save for the most basic film gag involving nothing more than a body moving within the frame.

In recent times there has been a collective critical effort from Cukor supporters to erase what they consider a dubious accolade, that of director of women's pictures, carrying as it does inevitable implications of soap opera, of miniature storms in middle-class teacups, of the lachrymose and the banal. They need not have bothered. Time and revolution have united to remove the sexist onus attached to the title. Ideologically, Cukor's films have aged much better than most of Hollywood's *macho* epics, come back from the Saturday matinees of our regressive adolescence to haunt our liberal consciousness. *Soldaten wohnen . . .*, smoker rowdyism, misogynist hawks entertaining the Hemingway phantasy of 'orgasm after orgasm on an island of peace in a world at war', as diagnosed by Leslie Fiedler. Women are a real problem to the he-man Hollywood director, and probably the best that they can hope for is admission to the sacred circle of the men without women, as vamps or tomboys or, worse, nice girls bent on unmanning the hero; as everything, in fact, except the real thing.

The Cukor values are best embodied in women, preferably American and contemporary; and yet, with rare exceptions such as *Susan and God* and *Her Cardboard Lover* (the titles are revealing), the Cukor world is not the unbalanced over-literal no-man's land of soap opera, any more than Mizoguchi's *Life of Oharu* or Bergman's *Cries and Whispers*. Even the world of *The Women* is haunted by the invisible presence or the inaudible voice of the male. Women are the centre around which the action revolves, but man remains the agent to spark off the process, assuming the role of 'engineer of feelings' (to borrow a little from Brecht) and presiding over the heroine's education. It must be understood that the process is seldom a romantic elaboration alone, and that man is never a mere sexual partner, an impregnator, a mere pretext for female modes of conduct. (The sheer expendability of the male in soap opera becomes obvious in films like *Imitation of Life*, *The Old Maid* and *To Each His Own*, to mention but three examples at random.) As a rule, Cukor finds his own special tone in a refreshing camaraderie between the sexes, in the crisp give-and-take of married couples, or in a growing bond of mutual respect.

Whatever they are, the heroines of Cukor are never the sweet, comforting creatures of Victorian fiction, whose final goal and fate is an epilogue of empty, safe respectability, the cosy glow of some perpetual twilight, so often transposed to the screen in an equivalent series of happy endings and fade-out kisses. The films of Frank Borzage and John Ford come much closer to this nineteenth-century idealization which is really an inverted form of misogyny: woman as the civilizing influence, the great domesticator. It's easy to detect the helpless Dickensian waif in *Seventh Heaven* and *Man's Castle*, stand-

10

ing for all the ancillary traditions of domesticity, and restraining their men from their restless wandering. With Ford, women come to represent the cultural influence at its most middle-class, the settling force that consolidates a violent, unstable way of life, and as such perfectly in context in period Westerns (*My Darling Clementine, The Searchers*), but a rather frightening virago figure in the modern context of *The Quiet Man* and *Wings of Eagles*. Ford shares the Dickens tendency to portray women as either schoolmarm angels or distorted grotesques. Cukor, instead, views his women the way Hawks views his he-men, at eye level.

Never the domesticating impulse to stand in the way of the male, the embattled Cukor heroine sets him wondering instead, questioning his superiority in a reversal of emotional dependency. The evolution, moral and dramatic, of hero and heroine is not achieved until the male has been humanized, chastened in some way or, very rarely, destroyed by the transformation he has wrought. The dumb broad of *Born Yesterday* acquires a social and political conscience from a journalist appointed to her education; his self-satisfaction will be shattered by her candour. Despite a bruised male ego, the coach in *Pat and Mike* capitulates to the ladylike amateur who has proved her superiority by winning every trophy. *The Actress* is nothing but a series of family crises that almost imperceptibly bring a father and daughter closer together. *Bhowani Junction* offers a straight dramatic reading of the same theme: an English officer sheds his racial prejudices through an involvement with an Anglo-Indian nurse of divided loyalties. The ultimate wisdom of Cukor's best comedies lies precisely in the muted suggestion of a Pyrrhic victory which subtly compromises the happy ending. The tactics of the courtroom extend to the bedroom in *Adam's Rib*, man and wife borrowing each other's psychological weapons to reach a romantic truce. Like Lot's wife, Gladys Glover looks back in the very last shot of *It Should Happen to You* at a world she is leaving (yearningly?, curiously?) behind. And all the romantic trimmings cannot quell the suspicion that Cukor, like Shaw, has no great romantic hopes for Eliza and Higgins; she having lost her place, however low, in the social scale, he his defensive armour of misogyny.

For most of his career, Cukor avoided the big statement. One notices a steady rejection of the tragic in his work (with the distinguished exception of *The Marrying Kind*), which goes much deeper

Born Yesterday: William Holden, Judy Holliday

than Hollywood's aggressive escapism of the first three decades of
sound. There is enough drama, the films seem to say, in the failure
of one-sided relationships (*Edward My Son*), or the inability of one
partner to grow (*A Star is Born*). Love or friendship or even family
ties are never understood as mere dependency or guidance of one
member by the other: *A Star is Born*, *The Actress*, *My Fair Lady*.
The ill-assorted couples in the marital dramas live through a series of
crises that bring on a final, painful coming to consciousness; their
story often ends in an impasse of fragile compatibility or a mutual
licking of emotional wounds. The husband accepts the wife's infi-
delity in *Desire Me* (in its original concept), *Wild is the Wind*, *The
Chapman Report*. The couple in *The Marrying Kind* reach a new
understanding after the death of their child.

This is the logical resolution of the Cukor male/female relationship rather than just compulsive obeisance to the happy ending. Cukor can organize our reactions to accept Norman Maine's suicide in *A Star is Born* as the final necessary step in Vicki Lester's emotional growth, just as the suicide (or accidental death) of Sylvia Scarlett's father becomes another trial in her coming of age. If the Cukor world depends on the partaking of emotion, the ultimate tragedy is then the refusal or inability to meet an emotional demand. The nymphomaniac in *The Chapman Report* dies alone in an emotional wasteland where there is no possible contact other than sexual; the mother in *Edward My Son* is driven to the symbolic suicide of alcoholism, being denied the affection of husband and child; Pursewarden in *Justine* fails to connect. Their deaths affect no one. Deprived of that reflected grace which supports the Cukor complex of emotion, they desiccate and die alone.

1: Broadway Beginnings

One cannot write about Cukor the film-maker without taking stock of his former career on the stage, for theatre helped shape Cukor's film style: his command of actors, his sense of dramatic nuance, his intimate approach, the inventiveness of his 'stage business', the ensemble quality of the acting, so distinctive in *Holiday*, *The Philadelphia Story* and *The Actress*, all of these derive from a long and successful theatrical experience. Most important, it weaves together Cukor's preference for female performers and the themes he developed later in his films. One should remember that, in our century, the American stage has tended to matriarchy, and that a single Broadway generation encompassed not only Bernhardt and Duse in their farewell tours, but such leading ladies of the English-speaking stage as Helene Modjeska, Ada Rehan, Julia Marlowe, Ellen Terry, Mrs Patrick Campbell, Maude Adams, Margaret Anglin, Alla Nazimova, Grace George, Laura Hope Crews and Katharine Cornell – Cukor himself directed Ethel Barrymore, Jeanne Eagels and Laurette Taylor on the stage – a roster that surpasses in number and lustre that of the matinee idols.

While the age of the actor-manager improved considerably the prestige of the male at the expense of that doomed, possessed quality best embodied in the Booths, and later in John Barrymore, an attendant hint of scandal still clung to women on stage at the turn of the century, exerting a vicarious fascination on their sisters across the footlights, the majority of the theatregoing public. Playwrights soon followed suit, releasing women from the musty grand manner of Sardou and Scribe, and the inexorable fate of a Camille or a

Butterfly. For, offstage slam to the contrary, Ibsen has left the door ajar for Nora and scores of restless heroines to escape from the doll's house of domestic conformity into a world of conflict and independence; and women conquered the stage long before they won the vote. Since then, there has been a woman behind most theatrical milestones, especially since a dramatic heroine now required less a noble rank than an ignoble past. In 1893, enter Mrs Tanqueray in the steps of Hedda Gabler, followed by a string of scarlet women, restless matrons, social outcasts, and the full spectrum of frustrated womanhood. *Mrs Warren's Profession* (which is running a successful chain of brothels) may have proved at first too pungent for American audiences, reared by Belasco on a bland theatrical diet of female imps and delicious little devils; but thereafter, actresses were rarely to play Peter Pan or *l'Aiglon*, as playwrights started offering emphatically female roles. Shaw alone displays a gallery of dazzling parts: Candida, Raina, Cleopatra, Jennifer Dubedat, Mrs Warren, Eliza Doolittle. (True, it's the playwright who speaks through their mouths, but there is wit and wisdom and a hard-edged practicality to these ladies.) Nowhere was women's liberation as clearly posted as on the billboards, the stage offering a splendid field in the battle for equal rights. In 1919, the heroine of Zoë Akins' *Déclassée* pays for her indiscretion by dying under the wheels of a taxi; ten years later, the playwright had quite a different ending in store for the gold-digger heroines of *The Greeks had a Word for It.*

A dual image of American women still prevailed when Cukor came to the stage after the end of the First World War. Already, the motion picture had claimed most of the male-dominated genres, such as melodrama, spectacles and Westerns of *The Virginian* mould. Every new season, the silents had claimed every stage success that would bear adaptation. There remained, however, a theatrical style impossible to convey without words. And, despite the successful efforts of Lubitsch, Mal St Clair and Henry d'Arrast, drawing-room continued to bloom beyond the reach of the cinema, perhaps, as Broadway snobs would have it, over the heads of filmgoers as well.

It was a theatre for a decade of economic boom, a slice of high life, blissfully unconcerned with social issues, mercifully free of poetic influence. The best of its practitioners were none but the spiritual children of Wilde and Maugham, the American cousins of Guitry and

Cukor (*left*) directing *The Royal Family of Broadway*

Verneuil. Still, the sound was genuinely American and the sensibilities those of the Jazz Age, with just the right hint of boozy innocence and smart disenchantment. Urbane, witty, permissive, idiomatic, not meant to survive its dead-right sensitivity to the moment, and drawing an enormous charm from the very quality of its evanescence. There is more to be learned about the manners, morals and states of mind of America in 1928 from a play like Barry's *Holiday*, which never aspired to profundity, than from O'Neill's ambitious *Strange Interlude*, aiming at a timelessness beyond its reach.

In the drawing-room pieces, the sexual restlessness of the period is refined into a 'modern' approach to such issues as marriage, adultery, divorce, sexual freedom and the double standard. If there was a desire to shock, it was usually smothered in good manners, the salon replacing the boudoir and reducing (or elevating) seduction and courtship to a polite contest between ultra-civilized people. The higher comedy became, the further it banished erotic involvement. Less rarified entertainments – burlesque, musical comedy, luridly exotic dramas like *The Shanghai Gesture* – retained an explicit attitude towards sex, but nothing neutralizes the sexual charge of a play like sophisticated badinage.

A theatre which so asserted the unimportance of money would barely survive the stock market crash, and Broadway knew a period of crisis while, to everyone's surprise, the movies continued to flourish on the thrust of their new powers of speech. The 'talkies' could use some of that urbanity which flooded the stage in the late Twenties, and drawing-room comedy was among the first to be exported. This essentially WASP world could not have been more alien to a largely semitic Hollywood; in comparison with the traditional, robust comedy proffered by the silent film, it was bound to seem rather anaemic. All those conversations over cocktails, that steady traffic from settee to fireplace, those genteel involvements, it all called for careful handling, perhaps also for a bit of broadening to make it acceptable to the filmgoer, without sacrificing too much wit or elegance.

All kinds of stage craftsmen were imported to supervise the transfer of the awesome theatrical past to the sound screen: George Cukor, Rouben Mamoulian, James Whale, Richard Boleslawski, John Cromwell, Busby Berkeley, George Abbot, Irving Rapper and many others. Actors, playwrights, musicians, choreographers, dialogue directors and voice coaches gravitated from Broadway to the new sound stages erected in Hollywood and Long Island, less perhaps for the promise of inordinate profit than for the chance to be seen and heard by millions, irresistibly tempted, as Donald Ogden Stewart put it, 'to bring maturity to Graustark', making available to the great American audience the best of Broadway. A good deal of the time they brought merely a large dose of snobbery and the brittle conventions that all too often pass for sophistication on the New York stage. Still, not a few were lured by the illusion of permanence which film seems to offer and theatre cannot, 'the chance for immortality' that once tempted Sarah Bernhardt to appear in silents, a medium that could not possibly do her justice.

Who cared then if the materials were a bit shopworn? In these first

17

days of sound, anything that talked was put into service. In Cukor's case, a Booth Tarkington satire of the Old South, an English chestnut about a lovable old grouch, a Hungarian drama resolved to end happily, or a farce of Barrymores rampant. The millions who had never seen or heard (of) Jane Cowl, Katharine Cornell or the Lunts were not to carp at the nasal 'Buddy' Rogers or the lisping Kay Francis. Many experts were engaged to teach the stars how to speak last season's dialogue, to drum some nuance into the untrained Hollywood voice, diction with tears. Nor was it always the language of Shakespeare, Milton and the Bible; and only very rarely the laborious word-blocks of Eugene O'Neill. Mostly it was the sophisticated patter of Philip Barry, George S. Kaufman and S. N. Behrman. Soon, however, everybody had to admit that those French windows creaked much too loud for the screen. For what comes across most clearly in these early days of sound is the invisible presence of the microphone, not that of the director.

Already established as an interpretative director on the stage, using performers for their maximum effect, Cukor was logically less attracted by the technical aspects of the motion picture than other, more expressive directors like, for instance, Rouben Mamoulian, who was to plunge into the resources of the new medium and exhaust them in a few brilliantly innovative films. It was not until *A Star is Born* in 1954 that Cukor allowed the *mise-en-scène* to come to the fore. Through the Thirties and Forties, apart from considerations of theme and style, Cukor could hardly be called an innovator. He is, rather, a unique refiner who limits himself to a few genres, developing such a subtle rapport between camera and performer that the $7\frac{1}{2}$-minute take in *Adam's Rib*, the one-shot sequences in *The Actress*, or the hand-held camera in *A Life of her Own*, pass almost unnoticed. For all their surface dazzle, the Mamoulian pictures appear isolated from each other, somewhat like stunts, linked (if at all) by stylistic touches. One looks in vain for a theme beneath the anecdote. But with Cukor one can always distil a series of correspondences, analogies and connections, a complex system that cross-references the entire *oeuvre* and refers one Cukor heroine to another.

Cukor directing Judy Garland in *A Star is Born*

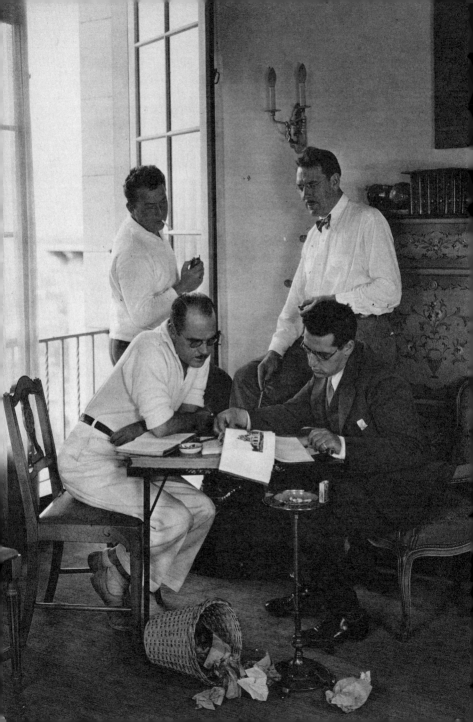

2: Stage into Screen

For a stage director of his stature and reputation, Cukor's beginnings in film were rather modest: dialogue director on two pictures, only one of which, *All Quiet on the Western Front*, offered any sort of challenge in a few highly emotional exchanges between men at war. At Paramount in 1930 Cukor was assigned as co-director to seasoned, second-rate craftsmen (Cyril Gardner, Louis Gasnier) in adapting three plays for the screen: he was expected to learn the intricacies of film technique while supervising the histrionic side of the production. The desired symbiosis, however, failed to take place in the first two films. *Grumpy* belongs in summer stock and remains fiercely stagebound, while no amount of directorial finesse could raise *The Virtuous Sin* from the level of a third-rate *Hotel Imperial*. Wistfully grasping at straws, one reads a signature of sorts in the polished bitchery of Jobyna Howland as the fussy, feathery madam in a Russian brothel at the time of Sarajevo. But a quiet absence of style informs both these films. Any of Hollywood's own directors could have done as well or as poorly.

Cukor was much more at home with *The Royal Family of Broadway*, a tart, ultimately sentimental tribute to a theatrical clan, a thinly veiled portrait of the Barrymores *en famille*. The film preserves the Broadway bias of the original Kaufman and Ferber play; it pokes fun at the vulgar, corrupting 'talkies' which have lured Tony Cavendish (Fredric March) to Hollywood and away from the family tradition which is the secular allegiance to the 'legitimate' stage. The domestic yearnings of Julia (Ina Claire) and her daughter Gwen (Mary Brian) are less treasonable than Tony's comic

Adapting *All Quiet on the Western Front*: Lewis Milestone, Dell Andrews, Maxwell Anderson, George Cukor

From the theatre: *The Royal Family of Broadway*

capitulation. Only old Fanny Cavendish (Henrietta Crosman) carries
on like a good trouper, accepting against doctor's orders the chance
to appear in a Brooklyn revival of *The Merry Wives of Windsor*.
Taken ill in mid-performance, she dies in her dressing-room, and the
heartbroken Julia steps into the role to keep the play going, thereby
realizing where her true loyalties lie and renouncing the idea of
marriage and a life away from the stage. The breathless pan and
crane shots that follow Tony's appearances are 'cinematic' in the
broadest sense, like March's performance itself. Ina Claire, on the
other hand, is observed in static, sustained shots, and Cukor is
simply but effectively conveying the antinomies of film and theatre,
in and out of the picture's context.

The following year, already a fully-fledged director, Cukor was chosen to guide Tallulah Bankhead through her talking film debut, *Tarnished Lady*. In what turned out to be a long if sporadic career, Bankhead's private quirks and public pronouncements were destined to overshadow her acting achievements. (In fact, she was properly served but rarely in each medium: *The Little Foxes* and *The Skin of Our Teeth* on stage, and *Lifeboat* on the screen.) In the early Thirties, she hardly conformed to the clear, well-defined images then favoured by Hollywood; and, since she could not be labelled and sold as either ingénue or vamp, the public saw her re-made into successive ersatz replicas of Garbo and Dietrich, then buried in hokum, such as *The Devil and the Deep*, *Thunder Below* and the sound remake of *The Cheat*. She might as well have stayed on the stage, playing Barrie and Pinero. At least, *Tarnished Lady* displays a Bankhead fresh from her London triumphs – Alabama and Mayfair vie to upstage each other in her voice – in whom there survives a trace of Iris March's gallant disenchantment. But the striking, unorthodox features call for the most flattering resources of a Hollywood studio, and the picture, in a naïve, misguided attempt to capture the pungency of its Manhattan locale, was made at the Paramount studios in suburban Astoria, well-equipped perhaps but incapable somehow of creating glamour and a mystique.

The story progresses, or rather regresses, from riches to rags, along the path trod often and well by Joan Crawford and Constance Bennett during the bleakest evenings of the Depression for the identification and wish-fulfilment of working girls everywhere. Bankhead plays a spoiled socialite who marries for money, falls in love with her husband (Clive Brook), deserts him to find self-realization in motherhood and a nine-to-five job, and finally returns to his side after he has been wiped out in the great 1929 Crash. In terms of popular fiction, the story stands as a modest draft for *Gone with the Wind*, divested of all the epic period trimmings. But *Tarnished Lady* glitters now and then with the profligate wit bestowed by Donald Ogden Stewart on better causes, most enjoyably in the well-bred matching of wits between Bankhead and a socialite rival, played by Phoebe Foster. Cast against type as the heroine's friend and adviser, Osgood Perkins is amiable and unromantic, even carrying sympathetic support to the extreme of informing her of her own approaching motherhood. This sexless other man, soon a recurring character in Cukor's work, offers more than subtle dramatic contrast. The part shows that the stage

Tarnished Lady: Osgood Perkins, Tallulah Bankhead

was infiltrating the less complex iconography of silent movies, which assigned a specific sentimental (read sexual) charge to each and every role, all neutrality deemed expendable. Thus the homosexual in *Strange Interlude*, neither villain nor figure of fun yet outlasting Nina's various men to voice O'Neill's ultimate comment on her life, all but vanished from the film adaptation made that same 1931.

For a while, the interplay between desexualized stage convention and the earthier eroticism of the movies extended the conflict between the two media in Cukor's style. Compare *Tarnished Lady*, which aims at the prestige of stage legitimacy (cast, author and director recruited from the East), with *Girls about Town*, which Cukor made in Hollywood immediately afterwards: a low-brow farce full of Babbitts and gold-diggers which displays a generous amount of flesh and lingerie incompatible with high comedy, but also a cheerful carnality synonymous with film vigour.

One Hour With You (1932), with Cukor performances in a Lubitsch context, is a charming comedy that either director could claim unreservedly, but one that nevertheless defies inclusion in either filmography, being too dainty for Lubitsch and still a mite too ribald for Cukor. Both directors share the same theatrical background, but Lubitsch's approach to marriage and adultery is essentially European. He is a peephole artist; doors in his films serve a higher dramatic function than merely admitting or removing a character, after the manner of the Labiche and Feydeau farces, or their Middle-European counterparts which so often served as inspiration. Both directors are aware of the importance of the actor, but Cukor prefers them in a drawing-room, while in the Lubitsch comedies (especially of this period) it is the bedroom one remembers best.

Cukor learned his craft at Paramount, but his career began properly at RKO, where he joined David O. Selznick after the legal dispute following his removal from *One Hour With You*, and its subsequent remake by Lubitsch himself. His first picture at the newly reorganized studios is almost quintessential Cukor. *What Price Hollywood?* traces the rise to stardom, and eventual downfall, of a pretty, ambitious waitress (Constance Bennett) under the tutelage of a film director, Max Carey (Lowell Sherman), brimming with alcohol, talent and self-contempt, the first and most vulnerable of a long line of Pygmalions. She crowns her success by marrying a socialite (Neil Hamilton), while her mentor goes steadily down the Hollywood drain, finally shooting himself at her home and, unwittingly or not, destroying her career.

Cukor's third film on his own is a well-observed, accurate look at Hollywood the Dream Factory, at that time still a patch of suburbia sprawling among the fiefs of the big stars and producers, an overly publicized small town bent on establishing not only a mythology and a cast system of its own, but an autonomous moral code as well. It is to Cukor's credit that the movie is relatively free of the supercilious Broadway cant which marred *The Royal Family of Broadway* or that other film about film-making, *Once in a Lifetime*; nor is it cast in the light-hearted mould of previous Hollywood self-displays like *Show People* and *Merton of the Movies*. The film aims higher: within the

Constance Bennett, Lowell Sherman in *What Price Hollywood?*

limits of affection and respect imposed by Selznick and his scenarist, Adela Rogers St John, it is the first sound picture to deal with some seriousness with the ethics of the star system. The passage of Mary Evans from private nobody to manufactured celebrity serves as a blueprint for the two subsequent versions of *A Star is Born*, but at a deeper level it was to haunt Cukor throughout his career.

For Mary Evans, the open sesame to stardom and fame is a banal bit of *echt* Coward ('Hello, Buzzy, you haven't proposed to me yet tonight'), her one line in a Max Carey comedy, her reward for seeing him safely home through a Hollywood premiere and another of his customary binges. Rehearsing at home until she catches the right tone of brittle insouciance, she is left breathless by this first glimpse of her own dramatic resources, a moment more ambiguous than elating. From this moment Mary is completely appropriated by the

Hollywood machine, and a Vorkapich montage charts her dazzling rise as 'America's Pal'. The same montage is later reversed when Mary falls from grace with the public. The effect conveyed in both cases is one of forces beyond Mary's control: rapid cutting, double exposure and fragmentation, all work together to cancel the performer out. Cukor also comments lightly on the heartless professionalism of the big studios in a sequence that recalls the famous opera scene in *Citizen Kane*, but in an opposite sense. Mary goes through her routine, singing 'Parle-moi d'amour' with great style and feeling, while all kinds of technicians go about their jobs with competent indifference.

The satire is not always that good-humoured. There are biting little truths about the film industry stated with detachment and precision. Max appears to have wasted his one considerable talent as a director just as Mary will waste hers in a series of tear-jerkers of the kind Bennett made popular in this period. Story conferences are neatly deflated. 'If you can't tell it in fifty words, it's not a good story,' contends the inevitable producer with a foreign accent (Gregory Ratoff, still a freshly minted cliché). The movie-going public is viewed with chilling ferocity. The wedding ends in a riot when Mary's fans hysterically attempt to reach her; the snooping of the fan magazines drives her husband out of her life; after Max's suicide, an irate housewife screams invective at Mary. The final, most telling irony is that a world thriving on exposure and notoriety should mete out banishment as the price of scandal: the violent backlash of Max's death sends Mary back to anonymity, now very much desired.

Constance Bennett's performance was Cukor's first unmistakable success on the screen. Ina Claire was, of course, the better actress, smart, humorous in her elegant way, the proprietress of a fine emotional range and a well-controlled voice. All she lacks is a real screen image: she is too static, which makes her look dowdier then than she did ten years later (in *Ninotchka*), while Bennett fills the frame like a Calder mobile, challenging the camera to match her gyrations and discover new, unexpected angles.

Searching through the vast storehouse of plays filmed and unfilmed, the Selznick people came across *A Bill of Divorcement*, an English play that, when first produced in America, had made Katharine Cornell an overnight star. This 'problem play', written by Clemence

Dane in 1921, was concerned with the effect of all those hasty wartime marriages on family and society. In a way, it could be termed a piece of moral science-fiction: in setting the action some twelve years ahead into the future (roughly around the time the Selznick version came to be made), Miss Dane envisioned a time when divorce would be legally obtainable as well as morally acceptable, a conceit not as old-fashioned as it may seem, since British law was slow to change and not until 1937 was divorce made possible in cases involving insanity. Precisely by bringing insanity into her play, the author was pleading an exceptional 'hard case'. Cukor and the adapters had the sense to realize that divorce, and not hereditary madness, was the contemporary issue in 1932, still carrying a heavy load of guilt, besides being emotionally more accessible. The ghost of Ibsen was accordingly exorcised.

The film still bears traces of the 'well-made play', the sort where church bells are stilled ominously when the telephone rings. Most of its contrivances are kept alive in the movie by preserving the rarefied ambience of the stage; except for two brief garden scenes, it remains doggedly indoors. It opens on a moment of precarious happiness in an upper-class English household. Margaret Fairfield is about to remarry, having just been granted a divorce from her husband Hilary, a shell-shocked war casualty confined to an asylum for the past fifteen years. Their daughter Sydney, a headstrong girl who has taken the family burden off Margaret's frail shoulders, enthusiastically approves of her future step-father, wasting no particular affection on the father she hardly remembers. Then, on Christmas morning, the Fairfields are informed that Hilary has escaped from the asylum.

A painful family reunion ensues, made all the more poignant by the fact that Hilary still wants his wife, while time has turned Margaret's affection to compassion and, worse, fear. For there are carefully hushed stories about other Fairfields suffering from mysterious maladies, and the family doctor alludes, in an off-guard moment, to the mistake of having children under the threat of insanity. The truth is that Hilary was, may still be, insane and not merely shell-shocked. Sydney now feels tainted, or at least capable of transmitting madness to her own children. When Hilary realizes the unhappiness he has brought on his family as a result of his regained sanity, he fakes a relapse to release Margaret from any moral obligation.

A Bill of Divorcement: Henry Stephenson, John Barrymore, Katharine Hepburn, Billie Burke

Sydney, however, sees through her father's play-acting: she allows Margaret to escape to her new life but she herself resolves to stay behind after breaking her own engagement.

As a film, *A Bill of Divorcement* succeeds only fitfully. Still, the trial-and-error achievement of a relationship between Hilary and Sydney furnished Cukor with one of his cherished themes. The sequence where father and daughter first meet neatly decodes the picture. It begins with his first appearance, a forlorn figure in trench-coat and hat, entering the drawing-room from the garden, bumping into familiar furniture in unfamiliar places before finding the nostalgic permanence of the fireplace, the camera tracking steadily away as if to convey the solitude of madness. There follows a complex set of movements that encircle Hilary and Sydney in separate orbits, the two remaining isolated within the same space until Sydney's tremulous 'I think I'm your daughter' reveals her presence and they are finally brought together in the same frame. This two-shot is sustained while they establish a clumsy intimacy with each other, and is suffused by an increasing tenderness in Sydney, missing from her previous scenes, where her determined stride, harsh opinions and masculine name evoked the notion of a substitute identity, that of the son once anticipated and never born. It is in this role that Sydney has gained her hold on the family, a role she now surrenders to become Hilary's daughter. There is another possibility, not the less valid for being melodramatic – that she intuits a shared bond of madness – and this ambiguity enhances the persuasion of their meeting.

In fact, Hilary is to Sydney what the alcoholic film director was to the heroine in *What Price Hollywood?*. They confer an identity where none previously existed. They also share the same tormented quality, which makes them stronger dramatically than their younger antagonists, the polo-playing millionaire or the genteel vicar's son. And their relationships are equally inviolate: mutual understanding makes all pretence superfluous, and they are not fooled by their respective deceptions. Perhaps Ms Dane would prefer us to think that Sydney chooses to stay with Hilary out of loyalty to the weak. Shaw sometimes takes up where Ibsen left off. (Doesn't Candida decide to stay home with Morell rather than follow Marchbanks into the world?) In the Cukor version, however, Hilary comes off as the one possible match for Sydney, a poet and musician of (now) impressive lucidity. The fade-out – father and daughter at the piano trying to complete the unfinished sonata of many years back – was at the time deemed unremittingly sombre. It now seems merely unconventional, Hilary's new hold on sanity balanced by Sydney's awakening emotions.

This reading of the play is a matter of performance rather than of any substantial revision of the text. Billie Burke, for instance, reveals what a delicate actress she could be, in the role of Margaret. A year later, for *Dinner at Eight*, Cukor established the character of a scatterbrained society matron that she was to play, with variations, for the rest of her career. But here, she is the embodiment of a woman sheltered by marriage and motherhood from the realities of life, and not a flutter or a *moue* is allowed to distort her frailty. Working with John Barrymore, Cukor recognized the tragic self-destructiveness in the actor, for Barrymore seems to provide inspiration for the direc-

Hepburn (with Billie Burke) in *A Bill of Divorcement*

tor's most desperate heroes, those who cannot survive their moment
of truth: the fading matinee idol in *Dinner at Eight* who actually dies
in profile like a hero in a Lorca poem, the actors at the end of their
emotional tether in *A Double Life* and *A Star is Born*, the suicidal
director of *What Price Hollywood?* (played by Lowell Sherman, who
physically resembles Barrymore), even the actor's own posturing
clown of a Mercutio in *Romeo and Juliet*. As Hilary, the familiar
mannerisms – the raised eyebrow, the overstated irony, the truculent
stare that conjures up Svengali and Ahab – are subdued to the
resolute seediness of the part. Throughout the picture, most notably
in the crucial speech about the absence of God and the black hand of
madness that reaches through the cracks in the floor, the legendary
resources of bravura remain mercifully untapped. And, if the two-
shots seem usually to favour Barrymore, he gallantly manages to

31

efface himself and divert our attention to the leading lady, Cukor establishing an ideal dramatic ground where the Barrymore grand manner can meet the determined modernity of Katharine Hepburn.

Of one of Hepburn's early stage performances, Dorothy Parker wrote: 'She ran the gamut of emotion from A to B.' With Cukor no further than a medium-shot away, it became the full range of motion picture acting, soon to encompass the irrepressible Jo of *Little Women*, the equivocal gamine of *Sylvia Scarlett*, and the matchless Linda Seton of *Holiday*. It was at the time of Hepburn's screen debut that James Agate commented on 'her raging ugliness and stark dissonance of speech', a virulence perhaps justified by the subsequent *Morning Glory* or *Christopher Strong*, but soon to abate with *Little Women*. Still, it is possible to gauge the impact of such jarring newness on the dramatic and critical establishments. The Benda Mask features posed a lighting problem only occasionally solved; at times, she is all cheekbones and elbows, but this flat-chested angularity suits the role of a slightly eccentric English girl. Wisely, Hepburn does not attempt a British accent, settling after a few clipped New England tones into comfortable stage mid-Atlantic. Agate's violent reaction to the Hepburn sound can be explained in terms of his Englishness and her Americanness: the disproportionate value placed on diction and musicality clashing with the most American voice the screen had ever heard (with the possible exception of Jean Arthur's).

There were, and still survive, more ambiguous traits to the Hepburn persona, not merely a very definite demand to be accepted as an intellectual equal which somewhat soured her appeal with mass audiences in the late Thirties, but also an androgynous quality that could at times escalate to a militant lack of femininity, a suggestion that she was capable of carrying emancipation on to emasculation, brilliantly exploited in films like *Bringing Up Baby*, where she was aggressively madcap, or *Suddenly Last Summer*, where she played a devouring monster of a mother. Hepburn, it was soon discovered, was far from being all things to all directors: she enhanced some excellent work by Hawks, Mankiewicz and La Cava; appeared with less distinction under Stevens, Minnelli, Capra and Huston. She also could, when misdirected, lapse into self-parody or, if the suffragette mannerisms ran unchecked, into bathos. (She played Mary Stuart for John Ford when she should have played the Virgin Queen.) Most frequently, and felicitously, she was to work with Cukor, and to what extent they influenced each other can be assessed from picture to picture.

Near the beginning of *Our Betters* (1933) an elderly dowager curtsies so low at a Royal Audience that her necklace snaps, scattering pearls all over the floor. Unable to retrieve them without loss of dignity, the old woman moves on. Next in line is Lady Pearl Grayson. She gracefully swoops down as she curtsies, retrieving one perfect pearl and, as the outraged owner gasps, she swallows it. The 1917 Maugham play thus receives a quick dusting, a brisk Thirties tempo, an updating of attitudes and sensibilities. For Cukor, it served as a preliminary sketch for *The Women* and *Two-Faced Woman*.

An American hardware heiress, Pearl marries into Mayfair society only to discover on her wedding day that her impoverished peer of a husband has married for money, and also has a mistress. Rather than jump in the Thames or run back home to father, Pearl becomes instead the most scandalous, extravagant and successful hostess in London, going as far in her audacity as to wear black to the Royal Audience. When her husband demands an explanation for this breach of protocol, she sends up Chekhov: 'I'm in mourning for your dead sense of humour, my dear husband.' The plot knots itself around Pearl's weekend party in the country. Among the guests is the Duchess, Pearl's best friend, confidante and eventual rival, an ageing, foolish woman, voraciously avid for the mercenary affections of a South American gigolo, Peppi. Pearl allows herself to be seduced by Peppi, is discovered by her younger sister, and inevitably news of the indiscretion reaches the Duchess, who becomes hysterical and denounces Pearl in front of her guests. (There is a fine unexpected reaction from Pearl, as she stands exposed but far from chastised. She turns to Peppi and purrs: 'You fool, I told you it was too risky.') The weekend deteriorates into an embarrassed ordeal, with a few of the guests valiantly trying to carry on as if nothing had happened – an effort described by one of them as 'engaging the pyramids in conversation' – while the Duchess tries to return to London, even if it entails the ultimate humiliation of riding in the luggage van.

To the self-made millionaire who loves her and subsidizes her way of life while deploring it, Pearl cynically confesses, 'If one felt about things at night as one feels the next morning, life would be a lot

Our Betters: (*above*) Violet Kemble-Cooper, Constance Bennett; (*opposite*) black for a Royal audience (Constance Bennett)

easier.' Having regained his financial, if not moral, support, Pearl devises an effective scheme to keep the Duchess under her roof and avoid the impending scandal. She sends for Ernest, a mincing lip-sticked dance master, the current rage of the smart set. As planned, the vacillating Duchess, all too eager to forgive Peppi for what is obviously a casual affair, surrenders to the temptation of perfecting her tango under Ernest's lisping, but stern, coaching: 'If you put down your foot, so help me God, I *shall* kick it!' Pearl has won the day and by morning the incident will be forgotten.

On the screen, *Our Betters* does not dwell long on the interplay of American and English cultures which Henry James exploited for all kinds of moral and psychological insights, and which Maugham mined thereafter for some facile irony. But then, two generations after James, Americans in Europe are no longer innocents caught

between New World values and Old World etiquette; already by Maugham's time, they had been succeeded by ruthless intruders from an unpolished, classless society, all too willing to accept the rules of the social game. Cukor takes what could be a Jamesian theme, the invincible superiority of the American girl, and refashions it into a display of upwomanship in Mayfair. From Daisy Miller, Pearl has inherited all of the audacity and none of the innocence. She accepts the corruption of her American principles less as the ultimate stage of refinement in her European education than as a welcome short cut to the single standard, becoming in Cukor's vision the New American Woman asserting her sexual rights.

Even for the permissive pre-Code period, a philandering leading lady who goes unpunished *and* unremorseful must stand as one of the great emancipated heroines. For a comparable directness in sex matters, one must turn to the Mae West character. Even before the season of austerity about to descend on Hollywood, it was also characteristic of Cukor to steer away from the more explicit byplay that often recurs in the world of, say, Raoul Walsh or Victor Fleming; although an American heroine willing to bed with a kept man out of *ennui* or momentary impulse would disconcert such lusty womanizers as Quirt and Flagg. The all-important seduction in *Our Betters* is rendered through a reaction shot of Pearl's sister. Most directors would grasp at the chance to visualize what Cukor resolutely keeps off-screen. In its place, he builds up the sexual tension, so that the outcome is not just inevitable from the dramatic standpoint, but visually redundant. Cukor is a director who has rarely resorted to that tired trope, the fade-out during the clinch.

The coming of censorship did not inhibit his style, but the films did not always conform to prevalent morality and several Cukor movies found their way into the Index of the Catholic Legion of Decency, the most famous being *Two-Faced Woman* (1941) which earned the distinction, then rare for a Hollywood picture, of being denounced from the pulpit. Even then, there was nothing to delete, the film abiding by the rules of taste and studio vigilance. Instead, two shots had to be inserted to remove the sting from the tale of a sensible young woman, unschooled in the ways of café society, who impersonates her own twin sister, an imaginary hussy of legendary ill-repute, in order to win back her straying husband. It is the Cukor motif also evident in *Our Betters* and *The Women*, from another

36

angle. And, for the moral standards of the period, a heroine driven to employ the same ruses that lured her husband to other, lesser women establishes a risky premise: that a woman is to be judged not only by her social graces or moral fibre, but by her sexual performance as well. It is precisely this discreet core of sexuality that balances the vague George Eliot aura lingering about certain Cukor films – especially in his middle Metro period: *The Philadelphia Story*, *Susan and God*, *Her Cardboard Lover* – where one is aware of a reticence in involving the characters in any but the most polite displays of passion. André Bazin argued that much of the Hollywood style was born of a lack of freedom. In Cukor's case, when the censor deletes some shots from *Bhowani Junction* or *The Chapman Report*, he is upholding the Cukor style.

It is a style where moral (or amoral) interests are inextricably bound up with manners. This ultimate refining of stage techniques calls not so much for dialogue well delivered as for silence and expressive behaviour. In *Our Betters*, as long as Constance Bennett is on screen rubbing cheeks with friend or foe, most of Maugham's epigrams sound expendable indeed. Visually, Cukor sums up the story in the most economic and persuasive of metaphors, when he cuts abruptly from Pearl, fragile and betrayed in her bridal white, to Lady Pearl, defiantly dressed in black at the Royal Audience. A whole film could be made on the change of heart implicit in this transition, and *The Women* is almost that, a satirical vision of the world as a huge powder-room, its denizens neatly classed as predators and prey. In *Our Betters*, the labels are much more subtle – for instance, Gilbert Roland's callous, languid Peppi – and the interplay more concise and intricate. Violet Kemble-Cooper makes the Duchess both vicious and pitiful, and much of the delight in this cruel, brittle comedy derives from the suggestion that, behind all the backbiting and bitchiness, a genuine, if tortuous, affection can exist between these women.

It was in his strict capacity as a director of performances that Selznick engaged Cukor to direct *Dinner at Eight* at Metro, but whether the studio's renowned conservatism or the incipient climate of repression came to bear, the film is not effective as a sexual comedy. It remains a comedy of manners, with most of the laughs at the expense of a newly-rich couple trying to crash high society; but most of the ironic parallels between upper and lower classes are lost

Dinner at Eight: Lionel Barrymore, Billie Burke

in the transfer, along with George Kaufman's mordant Jewish humour, which managed somehow to infiltrate and corrode the drawing-room antics on the stage. More's the pity, for *What Price Hollywood?* had already touched on the conflict between an older American aristocracy (represented by the husband) and the vulgar affluence of the film world, with the heroine enjoying the sort of privileged ubiquity reserved for actors in a tolerant society. (The abrupt change of status makes for hilarious rapport between masters and servants: Mary Evans addressing her Negro maid in Berlitz French, and getting a motherly 'honey' in reply.) By 1933, the New Deal had swept away the old Fitzgerald inferiority complex, and the very rich are not that different from you and me. For one thing, they had not been rich for long, nor were likely to remain so. In *Dinner at Eight*, the thin veneer of gentility that separates the upper class of the

Jordans from the coarse, plebeian Packards is fading fast in the wake of economic upheaval. The changing fortunes of the characters — almost too shrewd a cross-section of stock dramatic types — reflects a world gone suddenly unstable; despite the air of cloistered comfort in the sets and the patent disregard for the grimmer realities of the period, the film captures the social temper of the Thirties, some of its ever-shifting values. The social conclusion, as usual with Cukor, is an extension of personal values: the Packards, vulgar though they may be, will inherit the earth. Better an unscrupulous hussy with ambitions than a useless, parasitic wife.

The episodic structure discourages any ensemble acting, but there are some superior star turns which, more than the precision of each entrance and exit, give the picture its heightened theatrical tone. Already the takes are longer, each actor defending an allotted area of screen space rather than screen time. Marie Dressler's wonderful, improbable society dragon comes off best, because her physical bulk is used with fastidious, against-the-grain finesse. The down-at-heel movie star of John Barrymore, doomed by pride more than by age or booze, is almost too close for comfort. Even Lionel Barrymore and Wallace Beery are less blustery than usual. Playing the ex-chorine with social aspirations, all baby talk and guile, Jean Harlow scores as a comedienne rather than a sex symbol, without any noticeable loss of stature, as would in their time Marilyn Monroe and Sophia Loren. Sex symbols enjoy on the screen the sort of inhuman finality that excludes both change and growth, and Cukor's involvement depends precisely on a heroine's capacity for both. It is not surprising, therefore, that his most memorable performances were drawn from ladies of diluted, or ambiguous, sex appeal: Garbo, Garland, Holliday and Hepburn.

3: Versions of Literature

Having furnished evidence of an Eastern sensibility rather rare for Hollywood, Cukor was subsequently consigned to period pieces and literary adaptations. And such was the success of *Little Women* and *Camille* that for the remainder of the decade he was to bear the stamp of 'literary' alongside that of 'theatrical'. Very few directors, however, escaped the revival sweep. The past not only offered safe escapism to the Hollywood of 1933, already squirming under the combined attack of the pressure groups, but it was also free of copyright at a time when the studios were feeling the pinch. And behind these social and economic advantages lurked Selznick's dream and Thalberg's folly: namely, to lend movies a cultural cachet by going to the classics for a source that not even the most critical would question, or so they naïvely hoped. The ensuing and systematic looting of the library shelves was conducted as much to appease Will B. Hays as to gratify the Selznick/Thalberg literary ego.

Luckily, the cycle opened with a faithful adaptation of *Little Women* which was not smothered in reverence like heavier works to follow. It is a book that demands affection rather than respect and one that hardly deserves the sub-literary stigma amply earned by others of the Mauve Decade, managing to exist quite safely outside the nursery and the classroom, sustained by its whalebone-firm characters. Alcott herself knew and was influenced by Thoreau and Emerson, and her heroine is no Pollyanna or Anne of Green Gables, but a projection of her own partly realized, and contradictory,

Little Women: Jean Parker, Joan Bennett, Spring Byington, Frances Dee, Katharine Hepburn

longings. Jo March is the American woman about to burst out of the Victorian apron strings, the small-town girl who turns down the rich Fauntleroy next door, the New Englander who leaves home and kin for the big city and a literary career, and ends up marrying a foreigner who also happens to be a widower and father of five – one of the author's neat shortcuts to motherhood.

Admitting with some reluctance the Alcott craft, Brigid Brophy (in her essay 'On Sentimentality') takes her to task for favouring what she terms 'the direct appeal of sentiment' over the oblique one of Art. Cukor helps deflect some of the bluntest sentiment of the novel by imbuing his film version with a regretful wisdom, that of youth realizing for the first time that all things must pass. Even the passage of pinafore to bustle seems to carry its own regret for the doomed transience of childhood. At one point, Jo reproaches her older sister Meg for growing up too fast: 'Why can't we stay as we are? You had to fall in love and spoil all the fun.' Loving playmates one moment find themselves mismatched lovers the next, and in a narrative in which seasons leave an imprint on every scene, the film holds on to a precious summer instant before surrendering Laurie and Jo to the rewards and restraint of adult life. Death is also inscribed in the same seasonal cycle: the most redoubtable episode in the film (actually borrowed from *Good Wives*, a sequel), the passing of wistful, delicate Beth, is bound in metaphor to the migration of birds, and followed by an image that gracefully sums up the spirit of the original: Jo cradling the grieving Marmee in her arms, a significant and moving reversal of roles which asserts the continuity of family and life itself.

Even for Alcott, who died a spinster, marriage and motherhood are not the ultimate condition of womanhood, and it is all but impossible to render good women like Marmee and Meg interesting when there are no saving dramatic graces like a sense of humour or a rebellious spirit. Otherwise, Cukor's crisp differentiation of each character is on a par with Alcott's, notably Joan Bennett's scheming, thoroughly modern Amy. But the picture draws its strength and, better still, a winning touch of subversion, from Katharine Hepburn's Jo. Hardly the image of domestic conformity, Hepburn prevents the tale from wallowing in its own cosiness, cutting through sentiment with an infinite variety of laughs, capable of delivering whimsy like 'You're some punkins, Amy!' and still suggesting a sister under the crinoline to Dolly Bloomer and Susan B. Anthony. For all its high spirits, it is a carefully shaded performance that sets the mood and tempo for the whole film, the flutter and vivacity of the early scenes turning to a mellow gravity and finally reaching an almost Jamesian elegance, as when Jo rises from her sewing to join Professor Baer at the piano for her first taste of European culture, a heartfelt rendition of 'None but the Lonely Heart'. In an earlier moment, the Professor (played by a gentle Paul Lukas, as much a father-figure as Barrymore in *A Bill of Divorcement*) admonishes the budding novelist to seek her inspiration in the familiar rather than the fanciful (in Alcott rather than in Mrs Radcliffe, in other words), and Jo bids a tearful farewell to the last of her childhood illusions. It is a shot that Cukor sustains an unusually long time for this period of nervous cutting and widespread misogyny; and what demands this rapt attention from the director is the subtle but momentous spectacle of a young woman blooming into self-realization.

Success or failure in a literary adaptation depends on how far the film rises from the level of mere illustration to the text. The Dickens novels usually present their characters in a single unchanging attitude, without a chance to grow or develop, their only evolution inflicted by the passage of time as they get physically older or by the springing of a new plot twist. It is precisely this fixed quality, so well captured in the illustrations of Phiz and Cruikshank, that carries them through the many ramifications of the story without loss of individuality: these idiosyncrasies, this grotesqueness, are functional, acting as vivid reminders on the reader's mind to establish a continuity between serial chapters published at long intervals. But, as Dickens himself was first to realize, his characters have 'no variety of days', and the novels are short on emotional logic, 'all rotten architecture but beautiful gargoyles' as George Orwell put it. And perhaps Eisenstein's admiration for the sequential, cinematic quality of the Dickens prose was reinforced by this interest in caricature, this visual shorthand.

Most film adaptations of Dickens have failed either as Dickens or as cinema. David Lean's *Great Expectations* came close to success, partly because Lean is a storyteller of film, a tactful latter-day De Mille, but also because the book comes late in Dickens' life and displays a well-earned command of straight narrative, as well as dispensing with the repetitions that serve to re-establish characters in his earlier work. The problem is that *David Copperfield* is still too close to the Dickens of the *Sketches* and *Pickwick Papers*: its episodic narration sprawls over too many years, rambles over too many places and incidents, with the result that David is unable to emerge as the hero of his own story, an uncertainty expressed in the opening paragraph of the novel, which in the Cukor version becomes sad, literal fact.

Back in silent days, Griffith isolated a fragment from the book, the tale of Agnes and her patient love for David, to make a fine, if not particularly Dickensian, movie, *True Heart Susie*. In 1934, the budding 'Selznick tradition of quality' demanded no less than thirty roles of consequence, even if it meant reducing them to their trademark: Uriah Heep wrings his hands and drops his aitches, Mrs Gummidge moans by the fire that she is a lone lorn creature, Barkis

David Copperfield

is willin', and so forth. There is no time for shading, and ultimately the success of the picture hangs on the occasional felicity of the casting: the Murdstones, embodiment of mean, middle-class propriety, etched in deft acid strokes by Basil Rathbone and Violet Kemble-Cooper; Lennox Pawle as Mr Dick, a magical apparition from the Carroll rabbit-hole. As for the bumbling, ever-hopeful Micawber, some of that character's finer points may be lost in the vaudeville of W. C. Fields, which steers closer to Oz than to Boz; it is diluted Fields and not quite Dickens. But Hugh Walpole's adaptation culled some fine bombast from the original, such as 'You perceive before you the shattered fragments of a temple that was once called Man', or 'With renewed courage I again throw down the gauntlet to society', and these the actor makes for ever his.

At times, an image comes across with comic or dramatic impact, as when Micawber takes to the rooftops in flight from his creditors, the dome of Saint Paul's looming majestically in the background. Or Little Em'ly at the end of the jetty, the surf breaking under her feet, an ominous presage that the same sea will eventually take its toll. And, inevitably with Cukor, whenever a scene manages to over-extend its stay, it becomes genuinely moving. Aunt Betsy's denunciation of the Murdstones, or the unexpectedly touching farewell of Mrs Micawber, belong to that recognizable middle-range of emotion which is the director's province.

The trouble with Thalberg and Cukor's *Romeo and Juliet* is not that it follows the wrong approach but that it lacks any but the most cautious, being a straightforward reading of the play, unadventurous and totally oblivious of the complexities of the characters. One misses, for instance, the evil in the Nurse as played in familiar choleric style by Edna May Oliver; Basil Rathbone, as Tybalt, is little more than a sneer; the Capulet of C. Aubrey Smith an ogre. If there was counselling from reliable Shakespearean authorities, as the credits all too proudly assert, it didn't go beyond Granville-Barker, and must have been limited to the sets and costumes which manage to look both brand-new and old-fashioned, free of dust, sweat and cobwebs, Verona built in a day. Reinhardt's forest in *A Midsummer Night's Dream* of the year before seemed freely borrowed from Maxfield Parrish and was a much better place for it.

The text has also been pared to make room for the duels, the masked ball and the brawling in the square, all of which is intended to put the audience at their most familiar ease. But surprisingly, where the play races the lovers to their doom, the film keeps to a stately gait, in step perhaps with the ill-starred, miscast principals. Leslie Howard, the shabby-genteel charmer of *The Petrified Forest*, cannot suggest the fiery youth of the early Romeo or the lyric despair of the closing scenes. Despite a brave attempt, Juliet is beyond Norma Shearer's range; yet she does succeed in conveying the tacit duplicity attending her passion in her scenes with Capulet, subtle revulsion at the Nurse's suggestion of a compromise marriage, and fine, spine-chilling terror at the prospect of being entombed alive. These isolated fragments, insufficient as they are, attest to the unexpected rewards of the star system; for Barrymore, with all his

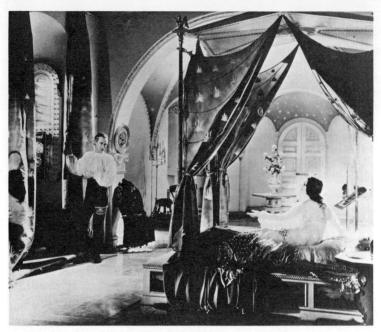

Romeo and Juliet: Leslie Howard, Norma Shearer

vaunted (if already declining) Shakespearean expertise, succeeds only in mincing painfully through Mercutio's bawdy passage.

When a major play like this fails to relinquish at least one sympathetic theme to the director, the result is an empty pageant. Many stage adaptations have failed just as lamentably. Historical plays like *Henry V* or *Richard III* are more assimilable to film. *Romeo and Juliet*, while nowhere as complex as *Hamlet*, still requires a degree of interiority, as well as a style to match the wordplay, to capture the oncoming darkness that settles down on the play after the death of Mercutio, or a way of rendering in symbol or metaphor the text's conflict of opposites – day/night, love/lust, rose/worm, alcove/tomb and so on – that finally asserts the inevitable presence of death as bridesmaid to the lovers. It must be said that recent versions have not fared much better, over-compensating in visual opulence for their

46

basic lack of interpretation. The Thalberg/Cukor version retains more of the text, and speaks it better, than any of the three versions produced in Italy in the past two decades. The fault with the Metro film is that, without a firm intellectual stance, the sum total of all its disparate elements adds up to naught. The musical score resumes rather than supports this *Romeo and Juliet*: where one longs for *Liebestod*, there is Tchaikovsky ballet music. Where there should be *amour impossible*, or any defined concept of love, there is only the same old faded Hollywood romance.

Not surprisingly both *Camille* and *Zaza* have gained new leases of life, however precarious, by being turned into operas; the plays themselves seem to exist mostly to display the performer's skill. The out-moded plight of their heroines, the aria-like highlights, not to mention the nineteenth-century notion of love-as-renunciation (which conforms so well to the Puritan ethic that it's difficult to grasp that these plays were once regarded as *succès de scandale*), all of this is best suited to the operatic stage – most conservative of dramatic forms, and also the most sympathetic to the showy bravura the roles demand. In the theatre, all this was quick to breed reaction, but Camille and Zaza remain recognizably truthful, in their way valid foremothers of stage heroines of less heroic mould, closer to Hedda than to Phèdre. To make them live again, in play or film, is less a matter of up-dating their sensibilities – as with the desperate modernizing of *Les Liaisons Dangereuses* and *La Curée* – than of respecting them.

To write about Von Sternberg without taking Marlene Dietrich into account – all too often a mistake among his admirers, certainly not among his detractors – is to render both a disservice while contributing to a dehumanized vision of the films themselves. To some admirers of *Camille*, it would seem pointless to discuss the film in any terms other than as a star vehicle. Conversely, it is the sort of film that invariably brings a tone of apology from the more recent Cukor exegetes, at most a passing recognition of the visual felicities of mixing Epinal and Daumier, or of the technical fluency that reveals Cukor at home in the medium.

On to Garbo. Her Marguerite is not exactly Gallic, yet a new, almost Latin verve tempers the customary *Weltschmerz*. The well-worn mannerisms – the untutored laugh, the knowing smile, the brow quick to furrow in wry disbelief or gentle irony – are

47

Camille: (*above*) Garbo, Laura Hope Crews; (*opposite*) Garbo, Robert Taylor

countryless as well as timeless. She now expands luxuriously, more graceful and agile than ever, unhindered by fullblown skirt or Sevigné curls. She does the polka, winks mischievously from a theatre box, draws multiple meanings from a fan. Even the flawless grenadier shoulders, here exposed by some flattering décolletage, loosen coquettishly or droop helplessly in despair. (Later, in *Gaslight*, there was a similar remodelling of Ingrid Bergman's healthy peasant stock into Victorian frailty.) And Bernhardt would pale at the timbre of this breathless, husky voice. 'Come, you must remember that I'm not the colonel's daughter just out of the convent,' she reprimands the prudish Armand for not sharing her heartfelt delight in an off-colour, after-dinner joke. This Camille doesn't know, or care, what a *réplique* means.

Garbo apart, one could still mine *Camille* for all sorts of minor

Cukor motifs, embodied mostly in the supporting roles. The chorus of predatory, fluttering *demi-mondaines* anticipates the menagerie of *The Women*. Rex O'Malley plays Gaston, Marguerite's devoted dandy, with the familiar tact and delicacy that stamp him right away as the Cukor Other Man, sympathetic and sexless. And it is quite easy to trace the genealogy of Varville, played with sardonic relish by Henry Daniell, from Murdstone to the scheming husband in *Gaslight*. But these are mere footnotes to the main theme, eventually to be developed in later works.

It is in the star herself that the directorial hand shows best. Cukor has choreographed her every movement, fussed over every background. A sea of black silk capes and hats for Marguerite's first entrance at the theatre, and an upward series of camera movements which convey her exalted position as the most envied and desired courtesan in Paris. The first love scene is staged in her boudoir, a quilted candlelit suggestion of a funeral chapel. After renouncing Armand, in another reversal of movement, she descends an ornate stairway on Varville's arm, a *couple maudit* in mourning, and the grace of her humiliation in retrieving her fan bespeaks the magnitude of her decline. The death scene is simple, uncluttered, the camera gazing down at a face that seems to register the faintest trace of emotion: hardly any lingering and none of the usual longwinded arias. Instead, life almost visibly ebbs away from Garbo, as the image fades into darkness, the film and the actress irrevocably one.

To the Romantics, love was woman's whole experience, and, depending on the actress, Marguerite Gauthier dies either a consumptive courtesan or a Romantic ideal. Neither seems to apply to Garbo's game, restless Camille, stricken not so much in the heart or in the lungs as in the very essence of her womanhood. Existing solely to be displayed, gambled away at the card table, her Camille goes from Varville, the man of property, to Armand, the callow young bourgeois, as if she were not even a sex-object but a token of position and wealth in a society which lives for self-display and seems to have forsaken desire. Richly ironic as well, and nowhere lost in Garbo's performance, is the fact that when the elder Duval comes to barter for his son's release, he is the only one to recognize in Marguerite — and appeal to — a sense of honour reserved for men. And when she affects a change of heart, dismissing Armand with a cruel, curt 'We don't make our hearts,' she is simply living up to a gentleman's agreement which, as a woman denied her own code of honour, will ultimately bring about her downfall and death. In this most famous tear-jerker of them all, Garbo is moving but hardly lachrymose, almost literally a Camille without tears.

With a similar tremor of the lids, theatre audiences who flocked to see Camille die came to watch Zaza discover the cosy, vulnerable sanctity of middle-class home life. Having discovered that her lover is a family man, she resolves in a surge of jealous spite to break up his marriage, but is instantly dissuaded by a touching encounter with his small daughter. Every great lady of the dramatic and operatic stage, from Mrs Leslie Carter to Farrar, seems to have left an indelible theatrical memory through the simple gesture of running an inquisitive finger along a lace tablecloth, a moment that somehow crystallized the then insurmountable gap between the world of the stage and that of bourgeois propriety, the grain of social truth in this antimacassar drama. Originally planned by Paramount as the American debut of the Italian diva Isa Miranda, the film was recast with Claudette Colbert, too vernacular an actress to suggest the holy beast of theatre Miranda would have made of the role (and eventually did, in a more modest Italian version directed by Renato Castellani). Instead of overwhelming the picture, Colbert fits neatly into it, enlarging the range she displayed in the Lubitsch and Leisen comedies. Abandoning all sophistication, she is raucous and vital as the can-can dancer of the early scenes, sensuous and emotional like an Ophuls heroine in the later stages. Colbert is, without question, a star; still, *Zaza* bears no trace of the star vehicle and is all the better for it.

Ironically, the censors of 1939 were as offended by the play's superannuated conflict as their forefathers had been in Belasco's day, which resulted in the removal of several scenes depicting Zaza and Dufresne in less than flagrant adultery. What remains is a stylish memoir of French music-halls at the turn of the century, a locale and period that anticipates *French Can-Can*. (There are other charming, uncanny similarities: Dufresne's baby girl confides to Zaza that her favourite fairytale is 'The Little Match Girl'; as Zaza waits backstage for her cue, the orchestra strikes up the Renoir standard, 'Lorsque l'amour meurt'.) What really binds Cukor to Renoir is a shared delight in the interplay of illusion and reality, as provided by theatrical make-believe and the fabricated self of the performer. It is in the theatre that Zaza finds refuge from her broken love affair, and where too she learns to incorporate a required touch of heartbreak into her art. In time, she becomes a grande dame of the stage, her own exquisite creation.

More than the early *The Royal Family of Broadway*, the film leads us directly to theatre as one of the main sources of inspiration in the director's work. Theatre in *Zaza* is not merely a closely-knit social group with rules and traditions of its own, even a caste system symbolized by billing, but also the one sympathetic milieu for an upward-moving heroine with morals and ambition far ahead of her time. Cukor's theatre films look upon the stage with an affection he denies to films (in *A Star is Born*) or television (in *It Should Happen to You*). These are latecomers to the world of drama – the fashion industry in *A Life of her Own* doesn't even qualify as such – and viewed as technical accomplishments or commercial enterprises, with little or none of the charismatic appeal of the stage. Nevertheless, it goes much deeper than stage-struck nostalgia. Jean Douchet, the French critic and film-maker, believes that all Cukor's films are in one way or another concerned with performance, whether deliberate or unconscious. It is perhaps too generalized a concept, although it is clear that the director enjoys extending the theatrical paradox beyond the limits of the proscenium by placing non-theatrical characters in a situation requiring them to act out a personal fantasy or assume a protective identity: social rather than theatrical play-acting. This is what makes the stage the ideal metaphor for the world at large, and Cukor the most Pirandellian of American directors.

4: The New Woman

To work from a literary source, Cukor evidently requires something that interests him thematically, such as the position of women in a male world, or the gradual transition of modern society from male to female sensibilities. All the more ironic that *Pride and Prejudice*, adapted by Aldous Huxley as a Cukor project, was assigned by MGM to Robert Z. Leonard. The revival craze of the mid-Thirties in Hollywood did not include any remotely controversial work, but then the task of the greatest Hollywood directors has always been to infiltrate the subversive into material approved as innocuous, or defused by the front office. Even within the self-imposed limits, one is free to ponder what *Washington Square* would have become in Cukor's hands instead of Wyler's. Comparing Cukor with Henry James may not be all that apposite, but there is a definite similarity in narrative form, and that illuminating technique of juxtaposing the before and after in a woman's emotional life, the 'double portrait' which is also the formal rendering of the Cukor process. The director may not share the novelist's talent for comparing different cultures and drawing rich irony or revealing parallel – although there are signs of this in *Bhowani Junction* and *Heller in Pink Tights*, even in the musical comedy terms of *Les Girls*. But in her actively modern manner, the Cukor heroine is 'affronting her destiny' just as much as Isabel Archer in *Portrait of a Lady*, and the angle of vision in most of Cukor's films remains as distinctively feminine as it is in James' novels. Perhaps the Cukor women are really expatriates after all, inasmuch as they venture with some emotional risk into a professional or psychological realm zealously guarded by men.

It was not until *Holiday* in 1938 that Cukor returned to the field of sophisticated comedy in what is possibly his most accomplished film of the Thirties. Already the subject of a screen adaptation in the early, premature days of sound, the Philip Barry play becomes in Cukor's hands a modern American fable, full of social and moral implications, delicate choices and unspoken kinships, a most Rohmerian film.

Johnny Case, an engaging young man with a healthy disrespect for money and tradition, meets and falls in love with Julia Seton, youngest daughter of one of America's Sixty Families, in appearance a kindred spirit to share his carefree, live-for-the-moment philosophy. She asks him home to meet her family, and Johnny's charm, as much as his theories, becomes a disquieting influence in the Seton household. The father cannot understand why Johnny, who has just made a killing in the stock market, should not aspire to a career in Wall Street. Both Ned, the son who is already an alcoholic, and Linda, the oldest sister, are instantly won over by Johnny's disregard for material values, his sane if iconoclastic attitude to life. When the time for decision comes, however, Julia takes her father's side against Johnny, being too sensible to overextend what to her has been but a holiday from convention. Ned is too weak and timorous to break away from the family cocoon; but Linda, who has gone from understanding to love, resolves to follow Johnny to an uncertain but irresistible future.

For its period, *Holiday* occupies a special aristocratic place in a Hollywood over-populated with more or less proletarian heroes and heroines tilting lances at the stuffy, snobbish, if not downright malignant upper classes (as invariably with Capra, from *Rain or Shine* to *Isn't Life Wonderful?*). Unlike the original 1928 play, the film doesn't set out to improve the public image of the wealthy; it simply assumes that class privileges can breed discontent, frustration and emotional repression as much as poverty and unemployment. Let Henry Kolker portray the Seton patriarch as a cartoon capitalist and the entire delicate structure collapses. What Cukor sets out to discover is the interplay of kindred sensibilities as they transcend social and psychological barriers. Like Renoir's *La Règle du Jeu* (which is actually closer to *The Philadelphia Story*), the film could not function dramatically had it patronized the lower classes or withheld a certain affection from its aristocrats.

In this pre-war period at least, Philip Barry remains Cukor's ideal source, the film-maker overlaying his own themes without once upsetting the playwright's dialogue. Cukor's favourite situations – the outsider breaking into an alien closed circle, and the heroine stirring into awareness, which are at the basis of the postwar comedies written by the Kanins – are conveyed in *Holiday* with grace and subtlety by means of twin, complementary courses through the Seton mansion, each floor defining a moment in the moral development of the characters. On his first visit, Johnny proceeds vertically from the kitchen level through vast, echoing halls, where he is ushered in to meet Julia, up to the warm intimacy of the playroom, the refuge of Linda's childhood dreams and longings (like Jo's attic in *Little Women*; but also, tinged with madness and obsession, in the sombre key of *Gaslight*), presided over by the fireside portrait of the mother who 'tried to be a Seton but gave up and died', a neat, unobtrusive Freudian touch. The same trajectory is later reversed when Johnny walks out of his own engagement party to Julia, an off-screen exit followed by a breathless Linda, the sequence coming to a fade in a close-shot as she stands framed by the servants-entrance, and receives a vivifying blast of Fifth Avenue traffic noise.

Not only is the dramatic conflict adroitly bracketed by these two similar movements, but a typical Cukor transfer has taken place, the emphasis shifted from hero to heroine. That the hero retains here an equal importance to that of the heroine is due, in no small part, to the fact that Johnny's grasshopper philosophy, so out of step with the earnest years of the Depression, has proved far from ephemeral. Cary Grant makes him the eternal dissident, the most charming and persuasive of drop-outs. At this stage of his career, he still projects the edgy, unrefined allure of the big city hustler, and luckily none of the folksy naïveté of his country cousins Mr Deeds and Mr Smith, both of whom swing closer today to John Birch than to John Doe, or for that matter, John L. Lewis. Katharine Hepburn's Linda, whether seething with spinsterish vapours or ringing out loud and clear her declaration of independence, restores to their classical proportion each of the often mis- or overused devices. The jaw is allowed to jut bravely out just so far and the mouth never droops as low as that of the mask of tragedy (or the pitiless Disney cartoon), while the voice – this time identified by a birdwatchful critic as 'a bronze caw' – seems to peel away layers of frustration from each line of dialogue.

Holiday may be the talkiest picture of its year. But talk never

Holiday: Lew Ayres, Katharine Hepburn, Cary Grant

dislocates the image, still a shade too neutral for partisans of eye cinema at all costs. It is civilized, witty, unliterary dialogue, without a trace of Pinteresquè undertow; and only shows its age in the few, muted references to Hitler and the New Deal. But Donald Ogden Stewart, who craftily updated Barry, had the good comic sense to place these barbs in the mouth of an irrepressible liberal couple, the Potters, played by Edward Everett Horton and Jean Dixon with the nimblest, most devastating wit outside of Robert Benchley. (As compensation for its 'dating', the film gains in hindsight pathos by preserving the original ending of the play, with the leads blissfully bound for Europe, hardly the promising Arcadia of Fitzgerald's era.) The Potters have been expanded into the mouthpiece of Stewart's political conscience; and so have the Seton Crams (Henry Daniell and Binnie Barnes) as their slightly sinister *alter egos*, whom Cukor

'The refuge of Linda's childhood dreams and longings': the playroom in *Holiday*

introduces with another marvellous arabesque that works both as exposition and hilarious indictment, as they walk up the stairs in one continuous take. The Crams are a pair of fascist snobs, but for the director their worst failing is the absence of humanity and that mitigating self-irony which redeems even the most reactionary characters in Barry's world. They stand for a social order in which names are more important than people: Johnny Case is referred to as 'Chase', which 'has such a smart banking sound', and the Potters are constantly misintroduced as 'the Porters'. (Horton, absent-minded but caustic: 'That's funny, I thought my name was Potter. I must have been wrong.')

Another director would have exploited *Holiday* for all its romantic possibilities. Typically, Cukor has shrewdly contrived to keep the couple at arm's length throughout the picture, with nary a kiss or a

Holiday: Grant, Hepburn, Edward Everett Horton, Jean Dixon ▶

passionate embrace between them, just a series of minute telling gestures that gradually bring them closer together, such as the way Grant presents his cheek for a playful, friendly peck; or a mock-romantic waltz by candlelight as a music-box tinkles away the old year – which skirts too close to the real thing. Cukor seems unwilling to furnish the audience with a purely romantic experience, as Borzage usually does (most notably in *History is Made at Night*), or as McCarey does in *Love Affair*, another emotional highlight of the period.

Two years later, when Barry, Stewart and Cukor teamed again to bring *The Philadelphia Story* to the screen, it would seem that they were betraying their former sympathies, the new film appearing at first sight as a perverse reversal of the values in *Holiday*. For here was the story of the rich girl who stayed home, married within her class and resisted the democratic urge to run off with a man from the other side of the tracks. Where the previous picture kept to the compact structure of the fable, the new one flies out in all directions with supporting characters and plot twists. Still, *The Philadelphia Story* explains and completes *Holiday*.

Once again, the private world of the rich is invaded by *agents provocateurs* from another social layer, in this case a reporter and his photographer girl-friend from a magazine aptly named *Spy*, both assigned to cover the marriage of Tracy Lord, a seemingly impregnable Main Line heiress, to a self-made man. In defence of their intimacy and with the reporters at the gates, the Lord family put themselves on display with the gusto of frustrated mummers (another echo from the playroom antics in *Holiday*). Uncle Willie is recruited to play the philandering father, Mother gently dithers, little sister turns into the family idiot, and Tracy herself into a sleek, hilarious parody of Katharine Hepburn, a dazzling act of forced smiles and brittle graciousness. Aghast, the visitors retort with a show of tough, wisecracking mordancy, the film becoming a succession of skits staged for the benefit of others. These are the moments when the Barry charm and the Cukor skill join without trace.

Gradually, the journalist loses his distrust of the upper classes while the heiress starts to yearn for a proletarian bold enough to knock her off the rather uncomfortable pedestal of her own making. On the night before the wedding, Tracy gets drunk and goes swimming in the nude with the reporter. The morning after, the groom draws the logical (if wrong) conclusion from the escapade; he makes the mistake of announcing to Tracy that he is ready to forgive her, thereby allowing his social ambitions to overcome his principles, and losing him Tracy's respect along with her hand. At the last minute, with a houseful of wedding guests and no groom in sight, Tracy turns down the reporter as well and decides to remarry her former husband and severest critic, a neighbouring playboy who would have her be as 'yare' (nautical parlance for fast, bright and easy to handle) as one of his sailboats.

Tracy, like Linda Seton in *Holiday*, is trapped in a social role which allows her no chance for the self-realization she yearns for. Dexter, her former husband, cherishes the memory of a younger and unrepressed Tracy, nude, drunk, sitting on a rooftop and 'howling like a banshee', an image of herself that Tracy has come to disown since it does not conform with her Puritan romantic principles. In her well-ordered world there is no room for Dexter's drinking or for her father's indiscretions. She gives her husband-to-be an unkind lesson in upper-class deportment by rubbing dirt in his brand-new riding breeches, training him to take his place in *her* society. (This is as cruel as the comedy ever gets.) Both father and ex-husband turn up on the eve of her wedding to undermine her confidence, repeatedly referring to her as either 'a virgin goddess', 'a perennial spinster', or 'that special class of American female, the married maiden', an ever-so-discreet suggestion that Tracy is not merely intolerant of human foibles but regards sex as the first and foremost among them.

As in no other film before or after, Cukor gambles everything on the players, the *mise-en-scène* being almost invisible in its discretion, a matter of glossy overlit sets and stagey groupings of three or four performers within the frame, all of which would soon pall were the performances not so mutually enriching. After a brief slapstick prologue which indicates another possible direction the film could have followed, the comic and emotional tension is sustained throughout by balancing the histrionic outburst with the breathily confidential interlude. James Stewart and Cary Grant are fine sparring partners for Katharine Hepburn. As the reporter, Stewart is free of his usual adenoidal mannerisms and cornfed charm; the scene in a public library when he and Tracy first lay down their mutual parody is quietly entrancing. As the husband, Grant fills out a rather passive

Sparring partners: Grant, Hepburn, Stewart in *The Philadelphia Story*

role with an over-abundance of mischief and urbanity. Barry wrote the play for the greater glory of Hepburn, and without her, Tracy doesn't play, at least not sympathetically. The play is beyond revival, yet the film remains one of Hollywood's most enduring comedies, a nostalgic recapitulation of a period. In *Holiday*, Donald O. Stewart had introduced some mild political bite, but no such reference is to be found in the later film; and, free of any timely ballast, *The Philadelphia Story*, made in 1940, floats airily back into the Thirties.

Between Barry engagements, Cukor directed *The Women* (1939) from the Clare Boothe play dedicated to the misogynist conceit that a woman's worst enemy is either herself or another woman, possibly her best friend and confidante; although, for all the play's vaunted cynicism, the playwright continues to palm off as worldly wisdom the old wives' notion that a happy wife should ignore her husband's casual infidelities rather than run the risk of losing him to a rival.

Nothing, or very little, remains of Scott Fitzgerald's adaptation on the film, except perhaps an excessive concern with the heroine's background and breeding which, since the play was acquired for Norma Shearer, was inevitable from the start. The final screenplay, by Jane Murfin and Anita Loos, is not only funnier than the original but tougher as well, even if as sexual comedy it still doesn't stand up to *Our Betters*. It opens up the action and takes it out on the streets; still, no men are seen or heard anywhere, as in the play, only now this unnatural absence establishes a sort of artificiality which Cukor sustains through countless short scenes and vignettes with a prodigious pace, while allowing now and then a few stinging truths about divorce and children. Where Clare Boothe, with malice towards all, pitched her sex-wise social climbers against an idle, useless upper-class, Cukor views both with amused affection. When a character threatens to overstep the limits of social comedy, as with Rosalind Russell's nearly pathological gossip, he plays it for broad double-takes and slapstick, somewhat like a female impersonator trying to crash the powder-room.

As in the Barry comedies, the elitism at work is more of the spirit than social, the most sympathetic character being that of the Jewish chorus-girl, played by Paulette Goddard as a cool connoisseur of men, rather than the foolish heroine manoeuvred by her intimates into a divorce she doesn't really want. Cukor almost makes a dull woman interesting, although Shearer's little acts of valour on the telephone are a little over-relished. By now, Shearer had suppressed whatever sexual magnetism she displayed in earlier films, like *A Free Soul*. She has become her own fantasy *grande dame* and cannot suggest, even discreetly (for the Hays Office is on the lookout), that married women must learn to hold their own in bed against possible interlopers, the way Bennett and Garbo did when performing variations on the role.

The manipulation of all the different characters – more than a hundred speaking parts, all sharp and clear – is in itself a feat of comic logistics, all the more impressive for seeming so natural. Here, style makes the woman, and a wisecrack defines personality. Joan Crawford, in an epochal performance as the hard-as-nails Other Woman, wheedles a rendezvous from the heroine's husband while a

The Women: Joan Fontaine, Norma Shearer

fellow salesgirl, Virginia Grey, delivers a running commentary on the performance. The upstairs drama is re-enacted in the kitchen by a snooping chambermaid with a flair for theatrics (Muriel Hutchison). The signing of a property settlement is supervised by Ruth Hussey, a study in efficient, unfriendly chic. As her sixth marriage dissolves, Mary Boland crumples on a sofa with a heartbreaking moan, 'Oh, *la publicité!*' Some of the dialogue ('Pride is a luxury that a woman in love can't afford') has changed in the intervening years from sheer soap opera to incitement to riot. But in all, none but the most committed, or humourless, feminist could take offence at this satirical contest in bitch hunting, the world seen as a vast female bestiary.

In 1941, reassured by the success of *Ninotchka*, the policy makers at Metro decided to democratize the Garbo image even further by starring her in a modern, sophisticated comedy geared to domestic audiences more than to the European markets which the war had closed. American film comedy, however, has a way of rushing in where serious drama fears to tread, and *Two-Faced Woman*, as the Garbo project was finally called, was denounced *ex cathedra* by the then Archbishop Spellman of New York, quickly withdrawn and re-released after new shots and dubbed-in lines had been inserted, with the result that the Melvyn Douglas performance makes no sense and that the delicate timing of the whole thing is ruined. Even after these alterations, the picture was still classed 'objectionable' by the Legion of Decency; scandal surrounded it and, understandably, it flopped. It was a different story when *The Moon is Blue* ran into similar trouble more than a decade later, dealing the first effective blow against film censorship and profiting extravagantly from the notoriety.

Now, the Garbo film seems funnier and even more adult and risqué than Preminger's milestone, although it is obvious that some heavy tampering has taken place. The screenplay (by S. N. Behrman, Salka Viertel and George Oppenheimer) makes Garbo a ski instructor who marries a man about town after a brief resort romance. Forgetting vows and resolutions, the husband resumes his job in New York as a magazine editor and also an affair with a mistress of long standing. The wife decides to win him back, not as her prosaic, sporty self, but as an invented twin sister, an irrepressible creature who dances with Dionysiac abandon and exults about the men in her life. In this guise, she easily upstages her rival and succeeds in bemusing her unsuspecting husband. Enter Spellman and the rest is history, or at least a final footnote to Garbo's phenomenal screen career.

Instead of a grand suicidal gesture, one discovers Garbo, spry and resplendent, delivering a double performance, first divesting herself of her usual mystery and glamour, on skis, in lounging pyjamas and even in a sensible, not too flattering, bathing suit; then, reviving with a comic vengeance the Garbo that once captivated the great American public, foreign, pansexual, all-knowing. Garbo drinking champagne from Douglas' side of the glass parodies a similar moment in *Flesh and the Devil* when she sipped the communion wine from Gilbert's side of the chalice, making one of sacred and profane love, and straining a few rules in the process. Like all good parody, it springs from affection, not from contempt, for the by now irrecoverable

65

femme fatale of the period between the wars. The script has her say, 'In this harsh new world there is no place for me any more', and the demystification is such that one reads it as a farewell, not to the screen as it turned out, but to the character. Nor would it seem premature if one considers Dietrich's fade-out of her Sternberg image a few years before.

What was 'objectionable' about *Two-Faced Woman* was the new Garbo, not the old story used several times before, once as a Constance Talmadge comedy (*Her Sister from Paris*, 1925) and often in such Cecil B. DeMille fables as *Don't Change your Husband* and *Madam Satan*, all of them adding a pinch of xenophobia to the spectacle of American-pie heroines impersonating the wicked foreigner. These versions usually gave the game away long before a serious issue like adultery was even raised; audiences could relax in the knowledge that Talmadge and Gloria Swanson could do no wrong. It was different with Garbo. The official condemnation of the film cited a sexual 'suggestiveness' as one of the main reasons, and no amount of tampering could erase it. The Garbo sexuality, not less real for being parodical, makes nonsense of the 'vertical ruling' on love scenes and bridges the distance between twin beds carefully prescribed by the Code. *En route*, Cukor scores a few sharp points on the compromise usually exacted from women by a marital impasse (Douglas making love to Garbo to enforce his viewpoint; Garbo fulfilled as a woman but frustrated as an individual), an unsexist view uncommon in the Hollywood of 1941. The old Garbo image having exhausted most of its currency when *Two-Faced Woman* came to be made, there are signs of another possible Garbo which hint not so much at the Duchesse de Langeais as at Margo Channing; that is, before a final second-unit ski chase rather gracelessly completes the unmaking of the myth.

I have deliberately left *Sylvia Scarlett* for a final flashback to the mid-Thirties, since it does not fit the pattern of either the literary adaptations or the comedies transferred from the stage. The literary boom found Compton Mackenzie arbitrarily lumped together with the whimsy of James Barrie and the juvenilia of Mazo de la Roche and Gene Stratton-Porter; it mattered not to RKO that the original *Sylvia Scarlett* trilogy once drew the admiration of D. H. Lawrence – he, of course, out of bounds in 1935 – and that Mackenzie strove,

67

Two-Faced Woman: Constance Bennett, Greta Garbo

Sylvia Scarlett

within his powers, to portray a plucky English girl on her way to modernity. The screenplay, by Gladys Unger, John Collier and Mortimer Offner, elaborates rather eccentrically on the one chapter in the first novel in which Sylvia masquerades as a boy to escape with her father, an embezzling book-keeper, from France to his native England. A written prologue to the effect that Life is but a Glorious Adventure is intended to condition the viewer to the sort of high-spirited romantic piece one would expect from John Cromwell or Richard Wallace or even the young George Stevens. Any of these directors would have complied. In Cukor's hands, the film turns out edgy and not always pleasant, full of shifts in mood and of implications that would have startled Mackenzie, and further delighted Lawrence.

The spirit animating *Sylvia Scarlett* is picaresque, not romantic: the heroine is confronted with a succession of trials and dilemmas which inevitably exact a price of innocence. Assuming the personality of an imaginary brother, Sylvester, Sylvia at first enjoys the deceptive liberation of the masquerade. 'Girls are weak and silly, I want to be brave and strong like a boy,' she announces, and soon after she is using her boyish charm on a susceptible landlady to avoid paying the rent (a scene missing from the final release prints, once again at the censor's request: other cuts and telescoping of scenes add to the jerky pacing of the film). Eventually, the *travesti* becomes a cruel joke on Sylvia for she cannot woo, or be wooed by, the man of her choice, and she is not wise enough to dispense advice in the manner of a Shakespeare or Marivaux heroine. Instead, she traverses the various episodes eliciting a series of ambiguous responses from male and female characters alike. Her father's mistress steals a kiss; Sylvia's partner in crime and on the stage seems ever ready to 'bundle'; the society painter she fancies admires her as a boy but ridicules her attempts at femininity. Before attaining maturity, before becoming one, Sylvia must not merely prove herself as a woman but perform as well a feat of courage and endurance proper to the male sex: she rescues a rival for the painter's affection from suicide by drowning.

Some episodes are not played for comedy: for instance, Sylvia cutting her hair in the opening scene to become Sylvester. (A similar action performed by the same actress in *Little Women* does not carry the same disturbing effect.) Others simply do not belong in comedy:

the gradual insanity of Sylvia's father and his final death are too starkly inserted in an already uneasy narrative. As performed, important characters compromise the romantic status of the project. Monkley, the Cockney con-man who is the film's nominal hero, is likely to join a band of revellers in jeering at Sylvia's father for his hopeless infatuation with a worthless doxie; his sceptical vision of the world as peopled by ' 'awks and sparrers', which Sylvia disputes idealistically, is nevertheless upheld in the fade-out against all romantic odds. In the role, Cary Grant sports a permanent five o'clock shadow and never once condescends to charm. As the painter, Brian Aherne is insufferably Byronic. One begins to glimpse Sylvia's plight, caught in the choice between the cad and the fop.

A failure at the time of its original release, the film has been rediscovered and, in recent times, made the subject of much Freudian speculation. But does it really improve *Sylvia Scarlett* to have all those psycho-sexual undertones? Are the unkindest cuts of the censor the most revealing? The romantic imagery is all there, in the fog-bound Channel boats and moonlit Pierrots, but *Sylvia* remains offbeat, the wreck of a romantic comedy. The one thing the picture can be safely said to be about is Katharine Hepburn. Like Garbo and Dietrich before her, she appears gifted with the two sexes of the spirit, Michelet's *sine qua non* for the true artistic temperament; a child of the century, bewildered and steadfast, all humanity and no gender.

5: Melodrama and Miscastings

The war finally changed the mood of the great American public: for Hollywood, the Thirties came to a close on 7 December 1941. Echoes of conflict, muted by distance and late in coming, proved nevertheless final. People going to war did not need to be reminded of poor little rich Tracy Lord and her insignificant problems. Attitudes that barely survived the Depression, the New Deal and Munich became tasteless, almost offensive overnight. By early 1942, a line like 'The prettiest sight in this pretty world of ours is that of the privileged classes enjoying their privileges' (from *The Philadelphia Story*) sounds less diverting than demoralizing, and criticizing manners and morals, even this mildly, risks undermining the morale. Wartime audiences must not be allowed to make the wrong connections. In Cukor's own *Keeper of the Flame*, hardly one year after Pearl Harbor, a very different Hepburn speaks some portentous line about the face of Fascism staring at her from across her own drawing-room. Epitaph for an era politely whimpering out.

For the duration of the war, comedy shed its better manners, along with its upper-class, and undemocratic, reticence, and some of its indoor pallor as well. Even the dark streak of Thirties misogyny, the spice of screwball and slapstick, was now transferred to the comparative safety of the thriller, a genre flourishing alongside the war epic and carrying the abrasive image of the madcap socialite to a further avatar, the deadly sex object. The hard-bitten Americana of Preston Sturges stands in splendid unpopular isolation during the mid-war years, a Capra gone sour, bent on resisting the coming onslaught of sentimentality.

The Forties remained a thankless decade for Cukor, a curious period that includes not only *Winged Victory* (1944), a wartime drama with long documentary sequences and the director's most marginal film, and the ill-fated *Desire Me* (1947), but also a series of melodramas. For Cukor, the genre represented new, uncertain territory, with its manipulation of character, its concern with shock and surprise, and its monochrome blacks and whites from which most serious directors longed to escape. Yet within the limits and co-ordinates of melodrama, Mizoguchi, Welles, Renoir and Murnau (to mention but a few) were able to develop all sorts of metaphysical insights; Sirk and Minnelli created perfect self-contained worlds; Chabrol and Hitchcock elaborated intricate moral systems. At first, Cukor seemed to approach melodrama as a somewhat devalued form, as if the proper and serious exploration of character and conflict belonged elsewhere. If he succeeds so well in *Gaslight*, it is probably because the basic situation could be, had been, rendered in terms of 'legitimate' drama; by Strindberg, for example.

Melodrama, for Cukor, became a dark declension of the male/female relationship. The first of these films, *A Woman's Face* (1941), complies with the demands of the genre all too literally by having the heroine remodelled not merely morally but surgically as well, with the role of man-as-catalyst split into two separate, almost Manichean entities: one the embodiment of all the destructive forces within the heroine, the other a plastic surgeon who removes the scar that had disfigured her face and shaped her criminal life, allowing the release of her long-suppressed humanity. For Anna Holm, the scar functions as a mask to conceal her emotions. She appears hard-bitten and cruel to the petty crooks who are her underlings, but secretly she indulges in such pleasures as music and poetry. 'I've read every love letter ever published,' she confides to her lover, the decadent Barring, who prizes himself a connoisseur of evil and regards Anna as a fellow damned soul. Barring can look at Anna's scarred face without flinching, her fascination for him residing precisely in her deformity. Once the scar is removed by a series of painful operations, Anna becomes uncertain of her new role. She has been given a new set of features but no corresponding code of ethics. Barring, who is immaculately evil, a true creature of melodrama, obtains for her a position as governess to his nephew, a child who stands between him and the vast family fortune, with the understanding that Anna is eventually to dispose of him. Yet, already on their first encounter, the little boy informs her that she will not be capable of carrying out the scheme: 'You couldn't be mean, you're too pretty.' To save her ward, Anna shoots her lover, a final liberating act which the script works overtime to extenuate. (*Born Yesterday* works better for transcribing the same basic situation to a comic key.) At the fade-out, Anna walks out of court acquitted, on the arm of the plastic surgeon who had once called her 'My cold-blooded, ruthless Galatea.'

Removed from the airy, well-lit drawing-rooms of *The Philadelphia Story* and *Susan and God*, Cukor plunges into chiaroscuro, low camera angles, semi-abstract courtroom scenes, a twilight world of shadows, neurosis and obsession. The one master touch of Expressionism, however, resides in Conrad Veidt's demonic Barring: Veidt has only to toast Satan to conjure up the whole miasmal world of the old German cinema, with its doubles and mirrors and pawned souls. All this is relevant to *A Woman's Face*, but nothing in the picture quite matches Veidt, not even Joan Crawford's fierce deadpan as the scarred Anna; and the two have their best moments when they are nurturing their sick sensibilities with the help of some fine florid dialogue from Donald Ogden Stewart. But once the familiar Crawford mask has been restored – a moment all the more effective for being so skilfully delayed – the *tour de force* is over and so is the director's involvement. What remains is the standard Joan Crawford situation and the bare bones of melodrama, the outcome clearly written across the star's unimpeachable cheekbones.

The very opening of *Keeper of the Flame* (1942), with its portentous lighting, reverent tone and intimation of doom, signals that this is no mere murder mystery but a political thriller, reshaped by Donald Ogden Stewart from a story by I. A. R. Wylie, and at times treading on *Citizen Kane*'s imaginative territory. In this, their first and least successful pairing under Cukor, Spencer Tracy plays a celebrated journalist and Katharine Hepburn the widow of a great American patriot, dead in tragic and mysterious circumstances. The journalist falls in love with the widow he suspects of foul play; she rewards him with the truth. The dead man was a potential dictator about to stage a fascist *coup d'état*, and his wife, who loved America and believed she had married a new Lincoln, let him go unwarned to 'a clean death in the rain'.

74

Keeper of the Flame: Spencer Tracy, Katharine Hepburn

There is no doubt about the sincerity and urgency of Stewart's warning, especially in the turgid days after Bataan and Corregidor, when the figure of Douglas MacArthur loomed alarmingly heroic; his sobering suggestion is that the same class that bred Tracy Lord and her charming circle could also bring forth a home-grown fascist leader. Tracy, as usual, is a tower of strength; but Hepburn, deprived of humour, gives a somewhat diffuse, overly cautious performance. (As Manny Farber noted, the fact that the fate of the nation hangs on her autocratic self-sufficiency is an equally disturbing notion.) The muted Leftism of the project outraged Louis B. Mayer and left Cukor uncommitted. Still, even more effective than the climactic statement is a sweeping crane shot as Tracy watches the funeral cortege file by, and rain-soaked mourners react with cryptic salutes and choked emotion, the image of a people conquered ideologically which sets off timely resonances of Prague and Warsaw. Cukor also views a patriotic Scout organization with a subtle disdain all the more effective if one recalls the Metro youth cult of the period. And there are vivid vignettes by Howard Da Silva as a resentful gate-keeper, Richard Whorf as a fanatically dedicated secretary, and Margaret Wycherly as the demented mother straying in and out of the past in her gimcrack parlour and proudly boasting that 'Big men have big houses and little people work for them.' Behind the widow's decision to destroy the man in order to preserve the legend lies the Borges theme of the traitor and the hero, the dichotomy between imperfect humanity and fabricated myth, and the various allegiances sworn to either. Here, alas, it is ill-served by Gothic excess and patriotic sentiment.

Thornton Square at night, the mid-Victorian era: bystanders and hushed whispers – a murder has been committed. Thus begins *Gaslight* (1944), a psychological piece devoid of all but the subtlest and most pernicious violence, the almost ritualistic destruction of an unsuspecting wife by her deranged husband. Instead of shock and surprise, Cukor works insidiously through detail and mood, usually ahead of the script. How long is it before the viewer, unfamiliar with the original play (by Patrick Hamilton) or the previous British film adaptation (by Thorold Dickinson), suspects the identity of the culprit? It matters little to Cukor, who gives it away almost from the start with jarring little touches, like Gregory Anton's self-effacement, the indefinable unease of his courtship of Paula Alquist, even an innocent enough shot of his hand thrust through a train window. The ensuing honeymoon scenes are more ominous, suffused with sickly period Romanticism, worn-out stones that lead to stagnant waters, a presage of darker hapenings which start to fulfil themselves as soon as the couple settles down in the old murder mansion.

The house is no mere element of decor but a third protagonist, upholstered, stifling, a closed world. Cukor's master touch is in the way he assigns various charges of tension to each level, and the vertical suspense this generates is uniquely filmic and disturbing. The attic bears down on the rest of the house: it holds the missing diamonds the husband seeks, and with them the obsessions and guilt of the past, pervading the place with a musty odour of murder and madness. The various levels always seem to define the characters,

shape their states of mind. As she grows uncertain of her own sanity, the wife retreats into her bedroom, situated directly beneath the attic, the *locus* of madness. At one point, she screams hysterically from the top of the stairs and is reassured by the unconcerned drone of the deaf housekeeper making her way up from the lower floors, which now seem as out of reach as sanity itself. And when the husband finally discovers the jewels, he forces open the boarded-up door that separates the attic from the rest of the house, an effect as shattering as that of madness suddenly unconfined.

Gaslight is mostly a relentless exercise in sado-masochism, as the man, with premeditation, deceit and excruciating efficiency, sets out to drive his wife insane. The film's most disturbing quality lies in the suggestion of an almost Gestalt dependency between tormentor and victim, a relationship that James Agee, at the time of the film's original release, criticized as morally questionable in the context of melodrama. Even now, the emotional pitch of certain scenes – the wife's brave little stabs at dignity cunningly undermined by the husband – renders them as harrowing as any current display of physical violence. But it should be recalled that it took Hollywood two decades after *Gaslight* to approach the Nietzschean 'deathly hate of the sexes' in other terms than melodrama, in *Who's Afraid of Virginia Woolf?*, reassured by the success of the Albee play, and on the brink of an age of permissiveness undreamt of in 1944.

The murder, the jewels, the trappings of the thriller are of less consequence to Cukor than the basic premise of a couple bound together by madness as much as by marriage vows, the husband attempting to remake his wife in his own image. *Gaslight* is less Expressionistic than *A Woman's Face* or *Keeper of the Flame*: Cukor must have felt that he need not resort to low-key lighting or oppressive ceilings, part and parcel of the genre long before Orson Welles filed an arbitrary but lasting claim to them. The force and persuasion of the picture derive instead from what seems at first an illogical choice of performers, especially if one bears in mind their predecessors in the roles.

Charles Boyer is in no way unctuous and effeminate, as Vincent Price was in the Broadway production of the play; nor is he fastidious in the manner of Anton Walbrook in the 1940 film adaptation. He may seem blunt by comparison; but by subverting the usual Latin Lover mannerisms, and alternating suavity with sudden bursts

79

of arrogance (which could be read as a mark of a lower social caste), Boyer is cleverly manipulating a very special phantasm of Victorian chauvinism, the sensuously corrupt and socially inferior foreigner. In Boyer's hands, the heroine's humiliation is both social (the wife discredited in the eyes of her servants, the musicale disrupted) and sexual (Angela Lansbury's Cockney maid as sexual paragon). Nor is Ingrid Bergman the gloomy, morbid creature Judith Evelyn made of the wife on stage, or the genteel housewife of Diana Wynyard on film. (Bergman's solid technique served her well in a variety of characterizations, but she remains the rare major star who never found her archetype.) Precisely because of her voluptuous figure and the healthy love of the senses she projects, Bergman's degradation is all the more painful to watch. It is a performance that Cukor has paced very shrewdly, for all its free-reined emotionalism; and even after the character has been reduced to exhaustion and dramatically voided, the actress can still lift herself to a final and exhilarating climax, when, aware of her husband's duplicity and the extent of his cruelty, she taunts him by pretending to be mad, a cathartic moment seldom found in melodrama.

After *Gaslight, A Double Life* (1947) seems only a series of theatrical notations, expert and amusing as one would expect from Cukor's first teaming with Ruth Gordon and Garson Kanin, but enhancing what remains strictly B-film material and was, in fact, the basis for *The Brighton Strangler* three years before. A Broadway matinee idol, a sort of Barrymore gone mad, so loses himself in his roles that he eventually commits a real, off-stage murder during an extended run of *Othello*. Regaining his lucidity in mid-performance, he stabs himself with Othello's dagger, and dies in the spotlight. This is the Kanins' one melodrama, besides being their only screenplay with a theatrical setting: while it has none of the smug conceit of, for instance, the Comden and Green libretti, it remains but a stage anecdote on a par with that of Kirby, the ham who died so magnificently that he took encores, which the hero spins with his dying breath, a trouper to the last. The unpretentious little thriller which first used this plot could hardly boast of such sharp insights as that bit of dialogue about all aspiring young actresses having played Claudia in summer stock. Otherwise, *A Double Life* rarely matches the simple suspense and sense of menace of its predecessor.

Cukor's long-delayed return to Shubert Alley is neither nostalgic nor respectful. By now, as with *Travels With My Aunt* a quarter of a century later, he can use a real location as if all the world were a sound stage; and no other director can capture so exactly the self-generating hysteria of a standing ovation. Otherwise, the direction is smoothly uncommitted, especially if one bears in mind Eliza, Vicki Lester and Gladys Glover, all Cukor heroines who manage a return to a former self. And except for Shelley Winters' 'dumb broad' waitress, the picture is untypically weak in the casting. Ronald Colman, as the actor/madman, plays with his usual rumpled genteelness; the soft, intimate aura about him is the specificity of the movie actor, Shakespeare being not so much beyond his reach as outside his scope. Some actors cannot be used against the grain (as Boyer was in *Gaslight*, for instance), and Colman was one of them. Cukor has him playing for charm and pathos, and even the inevitable shock of the obligatory murder scene is toned down, Colman wandering in a daze about the shabby bed-sitter until Winters unwittingly feeds him his cue, 'Put out the light . . . ,' which Colman completes, '. . . and then put out the light' as he drifts into his deadly Othello identity. In any event, American audiences of the mid-Forties, sensitive to the 'classic' reputation that Colman's radio readings had won him, made the film a success, and the actor was eventually rewarded with the Academy Award, an honour that must be extended to the director as well for his handling of what remains basically a miscasting.

The takes in *Edward My Son* (1949) are probably the longest in all Cukor. They encapsulate the text of the original play in sustained feats of performance and camera movement which correspond to well-defined acts and scenes, and are strung together by simple dissolves or sharply edited shots illustrating the passage of time or a bit of exposition in the dialogue. The filmic transitions heighten the theatricality of the main sections, serving as reminders of the more obvious techniques that the picture consistently rejects. As with Hitchcock and *Rope*, Cukor seems to be exploring the limits and points of contact of both media, but whereas the 10-minute takes in *Rope* sapped the potential suspense of the subject, there is a feeling here that Cukor might have succeeded had all his formal structuring been lavished on a worthier play.

Edward My Son: Deborah Kerr, Spencer Tracy

In the film, as on stage, one never sees Edward, who nevertheless palpably affects the dramatic development of the characters we do see. *Edward My Son* aspires to be the serious drama of a father's moral disintegration, and of a mother's physical and psychological ruination, the unseen son serving as justification when in reality he is a gimmick, an excuse for the play's rigid motivation. The play is mainly a complacent actor's vehicle. Robert Morley wrote it with Noel Langley, and was still playing the lead on stage when filming began at the Metro studios in Britain; it is easy to imagine the relish he put into the long asides to the audience, and into the escalating villainy. To this day, the film version remains filed away and forgotten as the worst miscasting in Spencer Tracy's career. There is no doubt that his American presence (in the film, the father is Canadian) upsets the social conflict of the original.

In the scene with the headmaster, when the father threatens to foreclose the mortgage on an exclusive public school unless Edward is re-admitted (quipping 'I'd twirl my moustache if I had a moustache'), the final effect is that of democratic pluck cutting through stuffy British class-consciousness. This could also be an improvement, and, elsewhere, Tracy's acting is forceful and cunning: the way he allows his usual bonhomie to seep through while still removing all trace of warmth and tenderness is little short of miraculous.

The heroine's decline from young unsophisticated wife and mother to dipsomaniac dowager could have been the most tragic evolution in a Cukor picture were it not so precisely posted in its development, so inescapable. Also, a short montage of vignettes, conveying through gesture and make-up the steady erosion of age and alcohol, makes most of the text superfluous. Deborah Kerr does well by the role even after her youth and naturalness no longer correspond to the character's, and it's not her fault if one keeps seeing the young actress behind the tremolo voice and the dowager's hump. It is a work of characterization rather than gesture or behaviour (very much like Maggie Smith's septuagenarian Augusta in *Travels With My Aunt*), and one that succeeds only when the context supports the grand theatrics, as when the pathetic wife derides her own weakness, moaning drunkenly, 'Champagne is rationed, you know ... by my husband,' while oblivious to a larger conflict, the London blitz, raging outside the window.

It has often been said, by Cukor himself as well as others, that no film as dependent on performance as his are supposed to be can survive a crippling error in the casting. But *A Life of her Own* (1950) overcomes the liability of Lana Turner's stolid, opaque performance and points to the all-encompassing *mise-en-scène* of the Fifties. Back in the Depression, the same story would have served as an optimistic Joan Crawford vehicle, a Cinderella fable to encourage a certain social arrivism. But the mood was different in the late Forties: for all its hard-bitten wit and insight, Isobel Lennart's screenplay is pessimistic soap opera. Lily James becomes the first Cukor antiheroine, a young woman caught in a series of circumstances beyond her control or understanding, drifting steadily towards despair and self-destruction. Furthermore, Cukor is impervious to the mystique

of the fashion world, which is shown, for once, with refreshing detachment.

He also refuses to inflate the material, to draw from a woman's picture a sociological statement about the American cult of success. Instead, he sidesteps the gloss and sentimentality which were as much an MGM trademark as the lion's roar. The Manhattan fashion mill shown in the movie is a world of cramped quarters, efficient bustle and specialization ('I don't do legs'). The grooming of a cover girl does not arouse in the director the stage-struck delight of similar scenes in *A Star is Born* and even *My Fair Lady*. It is just the kind of depersonalization against which Gladys Glover wages her revolt in *It Should Happen to You*, the comic obverse of the same anomical theme. (Lily's first lecture at the agency: 'All the graceful felines of the animal kingdom walk on their toes, only the bear walks like the ungraceful woman.') Lily simply becomes a marketable commodity in an industry that consumes youth and beauty at a fearful rate: the small-town girl out to make a name for herself in the big city finds herself a famous face without a name and, despite the pathetic resolve of the title, with not much of a life either.

Cukor loves his characters, especially the women, for their resolve and vulnerability, and also for their mobility. This time, uniquely, Lily's rise as a model is counterpointed with her decline as an individual. She has an affair with a married businessman but is not ruthless enough to inform his crippled wife. While the courageous little wife belongs to the romantic novelette since time immemorial, having Lily destroyed rather than saved by her sacrifice places the happy ending too arbitrarily beyond her reach. In a similar situation, Zaza falls back on a world of tradition and togetherness and there finds fulfilment as an artist. Here, without undue moralizing, Lily meets the fate awaiting the unself-realized woman: 'Back home in Imperia, they could tell by the way you walked what an awful ending you'd come to.' Lily's final suicide has been excised from the release prints (cut from 150 minutes to 110), and she is now last seen a forlorn beauty wandering the night streets, an easy mark for small-time sharpies lurking in cocktail bars.

As Lily, Lana Turner is much too passive: despite the obligatory hysterics and histrionics of the genre, she goes too gently into her dark night of the soul. Groomed and dehumanized herself, she at least fits Lennart's concept of certain women as a superb breed of

A Life of her Own: Ray Milland, Lana Turner

animal. Cukor's efforts are best rewarded by Margaret Phillips, a stage actress in her one film role, playing the broken Nora with neurotic intelligence; and, especially, by Ann Dvorak's has-been model, ravaged by insecurity, alcohol and drugs (the latter beautifully understated), a performance of gallows humour and genuine despair.

6: Comedy and the Kanins

After that first, tentative collaboration in *A Double Life*, Cukor was reunited with the Kanins for an almost uninterrupted series of six films, produced between 1949 and 1953, scripted by one or both, and forming as unique a body of screen comedy as that of Preston Sturges a decade earlier. The Cukor–Kanin pictures comprise four unqualified comedies, one biography, and a serious stab at that most elusive of dramatic forms, tragi-comedy. (Although antinomical directors, the parallel between Sturges and Cukor can be carried one step further: *The Marrying Kind* corresponds to *The Great Moment*, both bold, unpopular departures for their directors.) In his usual self-effacing manner, Cukor assigned himself the role of 'interpretative director' to the Kanins' 'creative writer'. Setting aside a ready admission from the writers that not only the director but the performers had a creative hand in the conception of the screenplays, one could say that the films, far from being mere transcripts, become the text themselves by virtue of enriching performances and dramatic resonance. They seem to re-evaluate in fresh terms themes already present in the director's previous work as much as they relate to Kanin's own films as a director, the late Depression era fantasies like *Bachelor Mother* and *Tom, Dick and Harry*, which purveyed the gum-chewing optimism of Ginger Rogers.

Kanin's work on the stage has been cited as basic inspiration for the series, notably his own *Born Yesterday* and a vintage Somerset Maugham play, *The Constant Wife*, which, incidentally, was directed by Cukor before he went to Hollywood. In his time, Maugham nearly perfected a kind of socio-sentimental conflict which never failed to give women their due. The heroine of *The Constant Wife* persists in regarding marriage as a legal contract in which both parties incur the same obligations and enjoy the same privileges; informed by a barbarous middle-class that this is not the case, she rebels and becomes a disreputable woman in everybody's eyes. Maugham's theatre had already played out by the Thirties, but his witty attacks on a social order which regards women as subordinates reverberate through *Born Yesterday* when Billie Dawn, illiterate mistress of a shady tycoon, discovers that the Rights of Man apply just as much to women.

In their own way, the Kanins were carrying the war of the sexes one generation ahead. As far as the text is concerned, a Cukor–Kanin picture is basically the story of how a woman oversteps the established limits of a given social system. It is indicative that *A Double Life* remains the only one of their films to take as its setting the theatre, to have a male character as the protagonist, and to be a melodrama. After *Zaza*, there is hardly any real conflict which could involve woman *and* the stage, and the struggle of the young Ruth Gordon in *The Actress* is waged against those middle-class prejudices that stand on her way to a theatrical career. The other social systems which form the background of the series – the legal profession, the advertising world, professional sport – are more likely to manipulate or suppress the heroine's aspirations than to fulfil them.

Whether written in tandem or separately, the scripts tend to disregard the restrictions of genre, sometimes overflowing indiscriminately into low comedy or high drama, the tone and verbal style tailored to very precise performers. Kanin's solo job on *Born Yesterday* (which Columbia officially credited to one Albert Mannheimer) is sharp, not too flexible despite its attempts at opening up the single set of the original play, and carries over from Broadway a typical smug alertness on political issues. *The Actress*, adapted by Ruth Gordon from her play *Years Ago*, is a straightforward memoir that never relies on one-liners, allowing instead a gentle humour to flow from the various relationships. Among the collaborations, all of them originals, *Adam's Rib* and *Pat and Mike* capitalize on the inevitable truce between the redneck paternalism of Spencer Tracy and Katharine Hepburn's outraged liberal sensibilities. The Judy Holliday films, *It Should Happen to You* and *The Marrying Kind*, abrasive, plebeian and with a flair for melting pot humour and

Adam's Rib: Judy Holliday, Tom Ewell, Jean Hagen

nuance, seem to have been written for the star's Kewpie Doll voice and Kosher delivery style; *The Marrying Kind*, especially, takes its tone from the breathless rush and the erratic pauses that seem to parcel a relatively neutral text into adjoining areas of absurdity and pathos.

The first of the series is *Adam's Rib* (1949), whose plot is too complex and familiar to bear repeating here in detail. It concerns the conflict between an assistant district attorney (Tracy) and his wife, a defence lawyer (Hepburn), as they clash in and out of court over the case of a housewife (Holliday) who has taken a few erratic shots at her two-timing husband. The lawyer-wife takes on the case as a chance to strike a blow for woman's rights; she pleads for equality, that the unwritten law be made to apply to women who take arms in defence of the home. The prosecuting husband views the defendant as 'a hysterical Hannah who tried to kill her husband', and his wife's court antics as a deplorable attack on the letter of the law and his own dignity as upholder of the same. She wins the case, he retaliates by framing her in a compromising situation similar to that in the case. Before the marriage breaks up, however, he wins her back by resorting to the most persuasive of feminine weapons, tears.

The rapping of the gavel becomes the three backstage knocks which traditionally signal the raising of the curtain. From the Kanins' sharp, sophisticated script, with its fine ear for class nuance and authentic legal lingo, Cukor draws a riot of theatrical artifice. In courtroom drama, particularly American, the establishing of an absolute truth is less important than the legal adversaries' capacity for performance. There is no one truth, only powers of persuasion. Hepburn's decision to dramatize an injustice implies exactly that: the courtroom as a stage, the trial as a drama staged for the benefit of an audience that comprises judge, jury, spectators and, ultimately, the film audience. The poor slob of a housewife is coached, costumed and even coiffed with a flower bonnet that functions perfectly as a token of domesticity imposed by the husband and rejected by the wife, so that she becomes a forlorn symbol of all put-upon and betrayed wives, past and present. Paragons of female intelligence, efficiency and strength take the stand, and Hepburn turns illusionist by conjuring up for the jury (and us) another variant on the triangle, which involves a sex change, the other woman becoming a suave, moustachioed homebreaker and the philandering husband a susceptible matron. She makes her point: morality, more often than not, depends on sexual bias and appearance.

To this broad courtroom farce Cukor opposes a no less theatrical but more stylish vision of the legal couple's married life. Here there is no theatre of the ridiculous but an illusion of the spontaneity and *savoir-faire* which we associate with high comedy. Departing from the screenplay, these vignettes are introduced with vaudeville cards ('And that evening'); at other times, the frame becomes an empty stage as the actors exit screen left and right. The only scenes untouched by theatricality of one sort or another are the grey, impersonal Manhattan locations which open the film, and the shooting of the unfaithful husband, done in flat, Louis de Rochemont-style so that for one moment we don't know how to accept it, despite the

Hepburn and Tracy in *Pat and Mike*

incongruity of Judy Holliday firing a gun at Tom Ewell. That the film is about performance of one sort or another is the point the critics missed at the time. They preferred *State of the Union*, made the year before, mostly because where Capra cross-cuts wildly to obliterate the film's stage origins, Cukor sustains a take for seven and a half minutes (one camera set-up favouring Holliday over Hepburn's shoulder), and transfers to the screen that most valuable asset of the living stage, the actor's moment of truth.

The other Tracy–Hepburn comedy, *Pat and Mike* (1952), brings them much closer to what Parker Tyler called 'the bathroom mirror image', easier, more relaxed and colloquial than ever before or after, in a film so smooth and seamless that it becomes very difficult to analyze in print. It is one thing to describe in detail a particular camera movement or the composition of a shot, another to put in words the essence of Cukor at its most understated, the way in which some of the best lines in the scenario are thrown away so as not to signpost the evolution of a relationship, unclassifiable by most Hollywood standards, between a ladylike sportswoman and a disdem-dose promoter who tries to make a champion of her; a fine romance, in the *Holiday* tradition, with no kisses. Hepburn's awakening is no longer a sensual experience or a crushing of her uppity prejudices, as in *Sylvia Scarlett* or *The Philadelphia Story*, but a democratization of her athletic skills, and instead of the kiss at the fade-out there is a simple, satisfying 'I need someone to look over me', and none of the wry recognition of mutual deceit that ends *Adam's Rib*. *Pat and Mike* appears to conform to a comedy pattern as old as its stars, or at least as old as their first teaming in *Woman of the Year*, but in reality it is more committed to character than to situation: Aldo Ray's punchy prizefighter, for instance, who is more affecting than laugh-provoking, another Cukor figure whose charm far exceeds his function. As for the sports *milieu*, perhaps not as congenial a setting as the drawing-room or the stage, it draws from Cukor a similar appreciation for ritual and respect for performance.

The four Broadway seasons of *Born Yesterday* guaranteed the canning of the play for mass consumption. The premise that you could not only take a whore to culture but even make her think had delighted the immediate postwar public, but by 1950 some of the more high-sounding talk about democracy and knowledge being freedom had fallen flat in the wake of the McCarthy witch-hunts. The tale of the crooked millionaire who hires a liberal newspaperman to tutor his mistress, an unpresentable ex-chorine, and then loses her as soon as she acquires a few elementary concepts, seems now one-third Shaw and two-thirds Damon Runyon. Whereas *Pat and Mike* flows, *Born Yesterday* moves along from wisecrack to punchline. There is Billie vulgar: 'You wanna wash your hands or anything?' There is Billie defiant: 'Will you do me a favour, Harry? Drop dead.' And Billie superior: 'You're just not couth!' For the screen, the play has been expanded with unobtrusive airings to several Washington landmarks, and expurgated as well. A line like 'He likes to get to bed early' becomes 'He doesn't want to share me with the general public', with some loss of Billie's forward sensuality.

Born Yesterday: Broderick Crawford, Judy Holliday

But even if *Born Yesterday* cannot but outrage the purists in the audience, it still fits in all sorts of cinematic observation within the rigid frame of the play. The first arrival of Billie and Brock at their hotel, he overtipping grandly, she piling up her fur coats on a hapless bellboy; the agile comings and goings in the split level penthouse, with its carefully subdued bad taste; neat touches of wardrobe and coiffure that have an independent wit, like Billie's black lurex evening number which clings to all places, right or wrong. The high points of the movie, as expected, find camera and director hanging on to the star's minutest twitches, unblinkingly recording the gin rummy tactics which demoralize Brock's game, or the overt passes which puncture the smug self-assurance of the tutor. One can almost see the dawning of an idea in Judy Holliday's saucer eyes, and rather than listening to distant laughter she has refined for the film her very personal mixture of shrewdness and stupidity, candour and cunning, moral sense and sex appeal. Opposite her, as Brock, Broderick Crawford overacts in distinctly filmic style, and

93

Domestic performance: Jean Simmons in *The Actress*

William Holden's ageing pin-up boy with glasses is recognizable enough to overcome any objections to intellectual heroes in films.

Not wishing to render unto Kanin what belongs to Kanin's wife, it would seem safe to ascribe to him the urban mordancy which is *Born Yesterday's* stock in trade, and to her the deeper emotional thrust that raises *The Actress* (1953) above standard nostalgia pieces like *Life with Father* and such. As in the original play, *The Actress* keeps in focus the selfish absorption of the adolescent Ruth Gordon Jones and her sometimes strained, sometimes touching attempts at communicating with her father, a cantankerous ex-seaman still chafing after twenty years of domesticity. But it also goes beyond the three walls of the stage to present an emotionally accurate portrait of the small New England town, *c.* 1913, which has shaped the lives of the characters, a world grown suddenly too small for Ruth, who yearns to become an actress. She is introduced in the balcony of a Boston theatre as she sits mouthing the lyrics to a song being performed on stage by her idol, Hazel Dawn, the Pink Lady herself. It is in such moments that *The Actress* connects with other Cukor films, like *Little Women* and *Zaza*. On one side of the footlights, the enraptured dreamer (Jo); on the other, the fake aristocracy of the stage (Zaza).

Whether Ruth will succeed as an actress is irrelevant to the film, which is more concerned with the sulky silences and sudden outbursts of a young woman coming of age and realizing that her own father also felt in his day the lure of adventure and knows all too well the terrible claims of family life. Throughout, the camera closes in on the characters, stalking them through the cramped, realistic sets in takes lasting up to four minutes. When Ruth performs for her parents, the staircase as proscenium, the camera takes in the touchingly awful performance without comment but is as attentive to the daughter's obsession as to the puzzled scepticism of the father, who rightly demands to know if the scene is 'a comical one or a tragical'. It is an admirable trait of the Kanin–Cukor films that they are infinitely considerate to their characters, all of whom have reasons of their own to act tragically or comically or both. The same balance of the sublime and the ridiculous is achieved earlier in the film during the Pink Lady Waltz number, with Hazel Dawn striking her graceful vintage poses, perspiration running down the livid, made-up features; or in the hesitating courtship of Ruth's young man, conducted to the steps of the *maxixe*. As the father, Spencer Tracy, for once deprived of partner or foil, underplays intensely his evocation of the joys and miseries of growing up at sea, and is raucously funny in an athletic drill where he loses his trousers along with his dignity. Jean Simmons refrains from making Ruth too gifted or too sweet, and is suitably moody and single-minded.

Although the credits list as sole source an original screenplay by the Kanins, it is evident on viewing *The Marrying Kind* (1952) that it must have been inspired by King Vidor's populist classic of 1928, *The Crowd*. The similarities are striking: the married couple in both films meet on an outing, marry, face hard times, lose a child in an accident, nearly break up, and hesitatingly agree to give their marriage another try. Vidor's hero composed slogans, Cukor's fancies himself an inventor; both feel inadequate to their more practical wives, who are a social cut or two above them. It is possible that some of Vidor's film became part of the collective memory of its generation; in any case, *The Marrying Kind* offers a reading for its

Domestic delusion: Phyllis Povah, Judy Holliday in *The Marrying Kind*

time: matt, disenchanted and much less sentimental than either George Stevens' *Penny Serenade* or Martin Ritt's *Pete'n Tillie* which also claim the same parentage. The very names of John and Mary in the Vidor film imply their universality, and not surprisingly it turns out to be the most Expressionist film of that director's career. While in *The Marrying Kind* Florence and Chet Keefer are as individualized as their names, they inhabit a workaday New York and not an urban abstraction, and are achingly commonplace rather than burdened with the mantle of significance.

In economic and revealing flashbacks, they relive their married life for a sympathetic counsellor prior to applying for a divorce. The soundtrack offers separate versions of their first meeting, conflicting reports distorted by ego and wish-fulfilment, while the non-partisan camera delivers the facts from a detached viewpoint, attentive to each personal delusion, to every casual quirk and squabble which will gradually erode their life together. Defenceless against tragedy, the Keefers are no better equipped to grapple with other realities of

96

married life. Each partner becomes an alibi for the other's frustration ('People hardly get to do anything'), and the death of their child, instead of bringing them closer, completes their estrangement. They are nevertheless bound by all the shared experience and finally decide to call off the divorce.

The Marrying Kind is not as serious as all that; it is, in fact, a little too funny at times, as if it were trying to promote Judy Holliday and Aldo Ray as a sort of middle-brow, naturalistic Blondie and Dagwood. Faced with a transition to drama unique for genre-strict Hollywood, Columbia Pictures had the film re-edited to emphasize the comic capers of the first half so that now, when the tragedy strikes, it is so abrupt that it catches the spectator as unaware as the characters. At a lakeside picnic, the Keefers settle down on the grass in a medium-close shot favouring Holliday, with Ray at her side, the children soon out of the frame to the left. The shot is sustained while she sings accompanying herself on the ukelele. Soon, it is obvious that something dramatic is taking place off-screen: people rush by from right to left, there is a hubbub, but the couple remain oblivious of it all until, at last, the older child enters the shot from the left with a shrill 'Mummy, Joey's drowned!' The camera is finally released from its fixed position to track beside Ray as he dashes through the crowd of onlookers, following him into the shallows where he retrieves the small body and brings it ashore. As the distraught couple bend over the child, the sobbing on the soundtrack grows louder, and a quick fade brings us back to the present, to Holliday racked with grief, and Ray's hoarse, exquisitely restrained, 'I don't know how we lived through it. Maybe we didn't.'

Yet there is no rupture in style: only the characters have led us from one emotion to another in almost a single sustained shot. Vidor capped an equivalent scene with a Germanic crane shot of the hero being swept away by a stream of passers-by, which reiterated the plight of man in a large city. There is no such arabesque in Cukor's film. Tragedy does not ennoble the characters any more than it does the film: the more hurt and vulnerable they become, the more they shout at each other and slam doors, and the homey claustrophobia of the apartment remains unchanged. The actors pull it off because they are still relatively unestablished, although Holliday tends to lapse occasionally into her 'dumb blonde' image; this was only her first film after *Born Yesterday*, and her presence blurs somewhat our emotional response to the split-second transitions. From Aldo Ray, virtually a non-professional, Cukor extracts his best male performance ever, all behavioural detail, gesture and inflection.

One of Ruth's girl friends in *The Actress*, unseen but mentioned in the dialogue, was one Gladys Glover, a name the Kanins borrowed for the heroine of *It Should Happen to You* (1953) and one destined to take its place next to that of another great heroine of American film comedy, Hazel Flagg, who in *Nothing Sacred* stands as objective correlative to New York's easy, morbid sentimentality, supposedly dying of radium poisoning but in fact just a small-town nobody on a big city fling. Gladys Glover, on the other hand, is both victim and beneficiary of Manhattan's typical, almost paranoid concern with celebrity, name-spotting and fame without achievement.

Gladys is a girdle model who loses her job and with it the little sense of identity she has managed to retain. Her name is scarcely more than an alliteration, and she is haunted by her own ordinariness ('It's not much of a name, nobody ever heard of it and nobody ever will'). What rescues Gladys from anonymity is a huge billboard in Columbus Circle which she rents with her savings, merely to have her name emblazoned across it. As New Yorkers take notice and wonder, a Madison Avenue firm that covets the location offers Gladys six other billboards in exchange. Soon, she is a household word that stands for nothing at all, being recognized on the strength of her name alone, featured in television panel programmes, selected as the model for an advertisement campaign, and invited to christen a plane named after her. By then she has gained some insight into her fame, and she tells her audience, 'I don't stand for anything, and that plane does, and you do. Why don't you name it One of the Crowd?' She finally goes back to the young *schlemiel* who loves her for her anonymous self.

In a picture nearly as manic as its heroine, every detail of dialogue, situation and characterization is concerned with anomie and identity, privacy and exposure, name and image; the first and best of media comedies, a film for McLuhan (Gladys fulfils a function as media fodder) and for Roland Barthes (she is a signifier without a signified, a mere denotation). The first glimpse of Gladys (Judy Holliday) is that of her bare feet wandering into the range of a 16-mm camera used by Pete (Jack Lemmon) to shoot a documentary in Central Park. She enters his life through film, and it's appropriate that, when

Celebrity image: Judy Holliday and billboard in *It Should Happen to You*

he later leaves her, he will say goodbye and admit his love in another
home movie, cinema being more persuasive than reality, and not only
for Gladys. 'What's in a name?' someone demands facetiously.
'Everything,' replies Gladys in all seriousness, realizing that celebrity
is in the eye of the beholder, not to mention the ear of the voyeur, as
with the Macy's saleswoman who squeals in delight at the mention of
the name, although the face that goes with it is unrecognizable. The
woman without qualities merely requires a little image fabrication
(echoes of Lily James in *A Life of her Own*), offered to the consumer
as the Average American Girl. 'A lot of penetration there,' says a
servile ad-man, while another ventures that Gladys is perhaps, well,
unusual. 'The Average American Girl is unusual!' exults the
executive who has hit upon this slogan. The media automatically
confer authority: Gladys is soon dispensing TV advice on such
momentous issues as dating and petting (If they're big enough,
they're old enough,' is her dictum). The film ends on one last lingering look at her beloved billboards, as Gladys and Pete drive past on
the road to matrimony and anonymity.

7: New Directions

Basically, *A Star is Born* is a rich retelling of *What Price Hollywood?* with the intervening years making fantasy out of fact and vice versa. In 1936, a second-string leading man named John Bowers, who had married silent star Marguerite de la Motte and whose career had declined, committed suicide by sailing his yacht into the Pacific. This local drama had been incorporated into the first version of *A Star is Born*, made at the time and glamorized beyond recognition. *What Price Hollywood?* had been reasonably sober and realistic in its depiction of Hollywood; but then in 1932 Hollywood was not in any danger.

In 1953, with television in the ascendant, *A Star is Born* became myth-making in self-defence and in remembrance of splendours past. The film celebrates, as it lovingly preserves for posterity, the ritual institutions of the gala première, the sneak preview, the Oscar ceremony. It goes behind the scenes in a big studio, yet it never exposes, it simply offers for our admiration and complicit recognition the make-up sessions, the wind machines, the cameras and the playback. This is first-rate fan magazine stuff, the collective fantasies of middle America; and there is no point in trying to pin it down to a date – it belongs to a state of mind which is ours as much as Hollywood's. Compared to the 1953 film, the intermediate 1937 version of the tale seems uninvolved and somewhat belittling, playing up the aberrant side of film-making and star-building. It never convinces itself, or us, that there is anything out of the ordinary about little Esther Blodgett from Smalltown USA. Anyone can be a star, all one needs is a break, talent comes later, bestowed by the medium itself; all of which must have fallen like balm on the bruised mass consciousness of the Depression. Remove the Dietrich eyebrow, wipe away the Crawford mouth, move closer and discover the girl next door. The new *A Star is Born*, on the contrary, is a paean to the one-in-a-million girl, a last burst of celebrant Hollywood splendour.

The film is as much about a real Garland as it is about a mythified Hollywood. It is her almost confessional, all-out performance as much as the CinemaScope screen which seems to dictate Cukor's new stylistic richness: for the first time in his career, Cukor is almost tangibly felt to balance the star's performance with his own. Take for instance the sequence near the beginning, when James Mason weaves his drunken way backstage at a benefit performance through pools of light which pick out from the surrounding dark groups of performers in contrasting colours as they await their cue, the camera tracking along at some distance from the action, and coming to rest on Garland in the act of adjusting her stockings. The blocking of the scene, with its combination of formal poses and unpredictable movement, the shifting distance from the action, the fragmenting of field of vision with props and obstacles, are designed not only to introduce the characters but the medium, to open up the unwieldy wide screen as never before or after.

Again, Cukor tries for the integration of seemingly incompatible genres, and succeeds: domestic drama, musical comedy and Hollywood chronicle cleverly support and enhance each other. Were *A Star is Born* conceived in other terms than those of mass entertainment, one would be tempted to borrow the Wagnerian notion of 'carriers of emotion' to link together the visual, the aural and the dramatic. Much has been made, first and foremost by Cukor himself, of the invaluable contribution of Hoyningen-Huene to the chromatic complexity of this and succeeding Cukor pictures. But one has only to view the colour schemes of *The Adventures of Hajji Baba*, directed by Don Weis and released almost simultaneously with *A Star is Born*, to realize that this is a case of artistic interdependence not unlike that of Welles and Toland. Hoyningen-Huene's subtle use of colour extends to the sets and costumes as well as to the photography: it supports the mood of the scene but never overwhelms it; it never resorts to the harsh, latter-day Expressionism of Alexander Golitzen at Universal, for instance; it never makes plot points but adds almost subliminal information on the characters.

101

Star ascendant: Judy Garland in *A Star is Born*

Despite cuts, deletions and the adding of a long aside in the form of a *potpourri* of song skits following the succinct 'Born in a Trunk', close enough visually to pass for Cukor's, the picture remains the definitive Hollywood apotheosis: larger than life, overly emotional, intelligent without being pretentious. It derives much of its power to move from the way its resonances are put to work, even in the music. Arlen's 'Over the Rainbow' has given way to 'The Man That Got Away'; the wistful nursery rhyme has become a torch lament for illusion forever gone. The credit for what is arguably the best song number ever put on film must be divided equally between the singer, the song and the director; yet it cannot be excised from the film without losing some of its dramatic power. This is the opposite of Minnelli's visionary musical fantasies with their sensuous suspension of logic and disbelief, and Cukor never allows the drama to coast on

A Star is Born: James Mason backstage

the bounties of over-production. As Esther/Vicki re-creates for her husband's benefit an abysmally absurd studio routine, 'Somewhere There's a Someone,' a lyric emerges from the frantic tempo and the underlying hysteria, 'With my someone/I'll be someone/at last,' which brings home the dramatic plight of the characters. James Mason's declining actor, carrying with him a secret loathing of the actor's condition, is a *magnificat* to the Barrymores of this world.

Cukor's other sallies into the musical field have been less distinguished. They turn up interspersed with the director's first spectacle drama and first Western, as colour and the panoramic screen seemed to open new worlds for him. Of the four musicals, *Les Girls* (1957), is probably the most conventional, with characters bursting out into song in mid-dialogue without the dramatic excuse of a film-within-

Les Girls: Taina Elg, Gene Kelly

the-film as in *A Star is Born*, or a show-within-the-film as in *Let's Make Love*. (*My Fair Lady* is in a category apart, as we will see later.) Some memorable moments in Cukor non-musical films are associated with musical numbers: for instance, Zaza singing her farewell to Dufresne under her gleaming white aigrette, or Gladys and Pete (in *It Should Happen to You*) casually drifting into an impromptu rendition of 'Let's Fall in Love'; both are integrated into the story and fit the mood of the moment and the characters. With a predictable musical number Cukor seems less at home, never quite accepting a transposed theatrical convention which on film blurs the line between the real and the illusory, world and theatre, however imperceptible the transition between the spoken word and the sung lyric, as it often is in *Les Girls*. He seems more at ease with the stunning diagonals of movement and colour in the title number, with

104

Gene Kelly's traditional hoofer introducing the act, than with the intimate 'Ça c'est l'amour', sung by Kelly to one of *les girls* in the normal course of their romance, and which draws from the director a familiar Minnelli crane pull-back at the beginning of the verse.

The songs, all of which occur in flashback, are part of each narrator's fantasizing. Even without them, the film could stand as a farcical feminine footnote to the *Rashomon* game of truth and consequences. There is no truth, everybody lies, Kurosawa seemed to say in his film. There is one truth, mine and that of my circumstance, counters *Les Girls*, however coloured memory may be by passion and prejudice. Kay Kendall and Taina Elg, as two members of Kelly's travelling revue act, offer conflicting accounts of their affairs with the boss, and it takes a third, Kelly's version, to reconcile all three to one all-embracing truth. Each version of the same situation, as visualized, does not contradict the others, a feat of ingenuity which is also an art of concealment on the part of the director.

The film as a whole is no better than its parts, for no musical comedy can rise above its material. The Cole Porter score lacks vigour, the Jack Cole choreography is notably devoid of dancing, Kelly is just another American in Paris, and the Mitzi Gaynor role is so underwritten that she doesn't even rate a flashback. Fortunately, there is also Taina Elg, funny, sexy and a good dancer; and Kay Kendall to work over a line of dialogue until it glitters ('I think I had a bad oyster,' she explains after an uproarious drunken evening). Looking like a malicious Gibson Girl, Kendall could have done justice to Porter's best vintage. Here she is left with the amusing, but minor 'You're just too, too'; and, briefly, *Les Girls* becomes the genuine thing.

In *Let's Make Love* (1960) spectacle erupts like an exciting disturbance after a reel of placid horizontals and brown monochrome. The billionaire hero (Yves Montand) attends a rehearsal, incognito, of an off-Broadway revue in which he is being lampooned together with Callas, Presley and Van Cliburn. (The plot may be immemorially old but the choice of icons dates the picture as exactly as its copyright entry.) The small stage in the Greenwich Village cellar is dark and empty; then spotlights brighten, and Marilyn Monroe, in black tights and bulky Shetland sweater, slides down a pole from some lofty region to wheedle and tease her way through Porter's durable 'My heart belongs to Daddy', while Jack Cole's athletic team bop and scat around her. It's quite the best scene in this otherwise amiable, rambling comedy with songs.

Expectedly, the billionaire falls in love with the girl, and she, believing him a starving actor, takes a special interest in his career and even gets him a role in the revue, impersonating himself. The poor man cannot even offer her a diamond bracelet without passing it off as junk; whereupon the generous Monroe passes it on to a chorus-girl; whereupon Montand has to retrieve it by hinting at the positively lethal effect junk jewellery has on the wearer. (The film's unexpected virtue lies in its relaxed attitude towards its lightweight material: the scene is a marvel of rebounding humour.) To become a song and dance comedian overnight, the hero summons the best talent in show business, and Milton Berle, Gene Kelly and Bing Crosby groom someone who is all thumbs, left feet and leaden sense of humour into a reasonable facsimile of Yves Montand the entertainer. The film is nominally a Monroe vehicle, but she seems strangely marginal to the story. What there is of her has been lovingly assembled from many short different takes (an unusual method for Cukor), and is a choice display of the familiar mannerisms in a different key than usual: the sex symbol as exemplar of all the homespun virtues, uncomplicated, generous with her affection and more than a little lumpy.

Cukor's one and only excursion into the epic, *Bhowani Junction*, was completed and released in 1956, the same year as *Lola Montès*. It's worth noting that, where Ophuls solved the problem of the cumbrous CinemaScope screen by reshaping the ratio with black inserts on each side of the letter-box expanse, Cukor plays according to the rules; yet we are never aware of a rigid shape, the screen appearing to contract or expand according to the intimacy or sweep of each scene. The picture is based on one of John Masters' scenario-like adventure novels, set in the India of 1946 at the moment of the British retreat. Needless to say, or this would not be a Cukor film, the wide, colourful canvas of railroad wrecks, riot and murder serves as background for the personal dilemma of a young Anglo-Indian nurse who must question her loyalties. The feeling of heat, dust, of red and ochre tides of humanity in a world in crisis, pervades the film. A simple transition scene, the climbing of a staircase, becomes a frenzy

Marilyn Monroe in *Let's Make Love*

Culture clash: Ava Gardner, Stewart Granger in *Bhowani Junction*

of solid diagonals and moving masses of people. At a train depot, hundreds mill about or lie down on the tracks in futile passive resistance to prevent the passing of a munitions convoy; readier to accept death than the threat of spiritual soiling, they scramble away when a cunning English officer orders sewage to be poured on them. The culture clash is as skilfully captured in the tiny reverberations of a limerick belittling half-castes, or in the tensely polite exchanges of an evening at the local cinema, where petty humiliations are endured with exasperated finesse.

108

Bhowani Junction contains some fine melodramatic scenes, the best in Cukor's career. Victoria Jones (Ava Gardner) fighting off and killing a rapist, as the screen becomes a chaos of steam, whistles and passing trains, and then a blood-red limbo. The most revealing scene, almost but not quite ruined by some over-explicit off-screen comment on the obvious, takes place as Victoria is about to betroth herself to an aristocratic Sikh, and the secular traditions of India appear to overwhelm the modern half of her nature, in an expert series of quick shots that ignore the rules and limitations of the wide screen. All in all, the director tells his story crisply and well, and the characters are still more than the usual stock figures found in this sort of fiction. There is a chilling portrait of a native terrorist from Peter Illing, devoid of all but the most ruthless fanaticism, for Cukor cannot bring himself to refuse him his reasons. He draws a lithe, sensuous performance from Ava Gardner, deftly enlisting some of her inconsistencies in the service of the dual identity of the heroine.

A woman's search for identity and self-respect is also the basis for *Wild is the Wind* (1957), a black and white Anna Magnani vehicle on which Cukor replaced John Sturges at the last moment. Inspired by a heavy-breathing Italian melodrama of a decade before, the film is also reminiscent of Sidney Howard's Twenties play *They Knew What They Wanted*, filmed three times, the last by Garson Kanin in 1940. An Italian immigrant rancher, widowed and prosperous, sends to the Old Country for his wife's sister, marries her, but persists in regarding her as a mere substitute for the dead woman. The new wife, who would rather be despised for herself than loved for someone else, eventually finds herself in the arms of a young shepherd who is the husband's adopted son. The affair is revealed, the lover banished and the wife, having won from the husband the right to be treated like an imperfect living being rather than an idealized memory, decides to remain.

The setting is a sheep farm in Nevada, and the locations have a vigour and open-air freshness worthy of Vidor. But it is the presence of Anna Magnani that provides Cukor with the firmest hold on what remains basically a predictable triangle drama. In this, her second American appearance, she is more gusty than tempestuous. There are the obligatory surges of Italianate temperament ('My name is Gioia!

Gioia!' she screams at her husband, 'Go and make love to Rosanna in the cemetery!'); but there is also some funny underplaying with a coin-operated drink dispenser, the kind of behavioural footnote that is worth a dozen pages of exposition. Two moments, without doubt, are anthological Magnani: in one of them, she retreats like a tired, graceless animal from the boisterous high spirits of her homecoming celebration to seek solitude under a nearby tree, and there she is joined by her step-daughter (Dolores Hart) for a luminous, almost wordless exchange of affection; in the other, Cukor restores to Magnani the gut power of earlier, coarser days in a one-take rendition of 'Scapricciatello', throbbing with the joy of release from the demands of both drama and the English language.

After thirty years in films, Cukor approached the Western for the first (and so far the last) time in *Heller in Pink Tights* (1960), in its way a critique of the genre. The picture was partly written by Dudley Nichols, who wrote *Stagecoach* for Ford, yet seems closer in spirit, and not too surprisingly, to *To Be or Not to Be*. Just as Lubitsch realized that the only way he could have dealt with the Nazi horror was to remain somewhat detached, to view the grotesquely tragic from the viewpoint of tragedians nearly as grotesque, Cukor utilizes a theatrical troupe to tour the Old West and re-evaluate its conventions and stereotypes.

The film is a Western all right, with even a beautifully staged Indian attack; but it is also one of the director's theatre films, like *Zaza* and *A Star is Born*, with the world neatly divided by the footlights. On stage, wigs, tunics, Offenbach and blood and thunder; the frayed European notions of love, chivalry and death. Off-stage, an audience of gamblers, hired gunfighters and robber barons bent on survival in a violent new world. The film pursues all sorts of sly analogies between the two. During a performance of *Mazeppa*, a hunted gunman peeks through the curtain at the audience as his pursuers close in from all sides. On stage, corpses pile up in profusion, performers declaim before dying, codes of honour and revenge are upheld. He finally makes his escape on horseback, only now he is riding Mazeppa's horse, bewigged and cloaked like the leading lady, leaping from the stage into the aisle, and disappearing into the night. This makes for a wry comment on the flaunted virility of the genre, but this is hardly a man's Western, having as its centre a

111

Wild is the Wind: Anna Magnani, Anthony Quinn

Heller in Pink Tights: Sophia Loren

recalcitrant heroine, played by Sophia Loren, who looks and acts like a Seurat figure stranded in an Old West print.

Cukor's worst-fated film of this period is *The Chapman Report* (1962), adapted from the Irving Wallace best-seller which at the time profited from the attention and controversy surrounding the disclosures of the Kinsey Report on American sexual behaviour. The film was recut by producer Darryl F. Zanuck against the director's wishes, then further mangled by the censors who regarded it as sexploitation (which the book certainly was), and there remain but gleaming fragments of the original, unbalanced certainly yet far from inconclusive.

There is no doubt that Cukor approached his source material with considerable caution and that he lavished effort and affection on the contrapuntal effect of the four case histories that comprise the story-line, and which have been altered by the re-editing and the cuts. (For one thing, the irritating comic relief did not loom so intrusively in the original.) Fortunately for us, no amount of trafficking could damage a system of expressive visuals comparable to Minnelli's, where 'packets' of colour are employed as in *Les Girls* to establish the emotional background of each character, even to define their predicament: Jane Fonda's immaculate white dress and the flesh tones of Claire Bloom's bedroom reflect the frigidity of one and the nymphomania of the other, and also their pathetic inadequacy to cope with their problems. And the sustained take being the Cukor stylistic unit, it is still possible to reconstruct the original from the few of them that remain intact.

This is a film about women under stress, sharing in the social ritual but living in a world of secret thoughts. One is a suburban Bovary (Shelley Winters) married to a well-meaning clod and conducting an affair with a younger man. Another repudiates sex (Jane Fonda) and has sought sublimation in a father–daughter relationship. A third (Glynis Johns) dabbles in acting, painting and adultery without much success in any. The last (Claire Bloom) is a nymphomaniac divorcee. A two-man team of sexual researchers comes to the upper-class suburb where they live, the women consent to be interviewed on a nearly confessional basis, and this leads up to a chain reaction of emotional crises.

Sex, and the guilt that results from its denial or excess, dominates the lives of the four women. We watch them react to the impersonal prodding. Fonda becomes vehemently defensive, bursting out with 'Why do you have to put so much emphasis on physical love?' On the other hand, Winters is consumed by shame as she tearfully admits to a sexual need her husband could not possibly comprehend or satisfy. Johns feels mildly aroused by the questioning and resolves to have a fling with a beach bum, while Bloom reacts by stepping around the partition that separates her from the unseen inquisitor, and which guarantees anonymity for both. All are observed without malice or irony; this the film reserves for the investigators. For Chapman, women are reduced to codes, numbers and statistics. A more traditional viewpoint upheld by the local physician (and Henry Daniell's physique prevents us from identifying with his views on sex, love and guilt, however liberal they seem) would regard some of

'Desperate intimacies': Claire Bloom in *The Chapman Report*

the cases as pathological. Cukor allows himself a telling comment on both views as the men exhibit a certain professional satisfaction at having their diagnoses confirmed by the nymphomaniac's eventual suicide.

The women are much more complex than any of their respective dogmas will admit. It is a matter of point of view; that is, of camera placement. Interviewer and subject are introduced in separate medium shots which make for empathy, until a long shot reveals the partition that prevents any commitment on a purely human level. It's quite obvious that for Cukor the nymphomaniac is the most complex of the four characters, being the most feminine as well as the most 'virile', for she alone decides to terminate the false intimacy of the research sessions to be on an equal standing with the investigator. Earlier in the story, she confronts her mirror-image in the person of a randy, brutal neighbour, and through a wire-mesh door that resembles a mirror her desire almost matches his. Like her male counterparts in *What Price Hollywood?*, *Dinner at Eight* and *A Star is Born*, she seeks the truth in her mirror and cannot bear what she sees.

At times, the reshuffling of the various episodes makes for some blunt juxtapositions, as when Bloom's tragic mask lap-dissolves into Glynis Johns twittering away as she prepares for her tryst with a prospective lover. And if Cukor appears to patronize the arty, ridiculous character she plays, which is indeed rare for the director, it may be because of all four heroines she alone has no *daemon*, no serious psychic flaw. Not by accident her scenes are drenched in light, while Fonda, Winters and Bloom seem to drift constantly from a high-definition social context to shadowed areas where desperate intimacies take place; there is, for instance, a unique interplay of physical desire, provocation and self-loathing in the scene where Bloom attempts to seduce a water-delivery boy (Chad Everett). Unknown to each other, these characters are treading the same dark ground, and the film makes it clear that their special truth escapes cataloguing on the other side of that man-made partition. One need not go as far as *Valley of the Dolls* to realize how well Cukor succeeded.

'By George, Eliza, the streets will be strewn with the bodies of men shooting themselves for your sake before I've done with you.' One would imagine Shaw's *Pygmalion* the ideal formulation of all the themes so dear to Cukor, with its forceful confrontation, tinged with wit and Shaw's own bachelor perversity, between Higgins and Eliza, almost exemplary surrogates for the director and his actress. For the 1938 film adaptation, Shaw had mellowed enough to include in his screenplay some hope of romance in the dialectic involvement of the phonetician and the flower-girl he teaches to speak like a duchess. All this has been well-nigh supplanted in the mind and memories of theatre and filmgoers by the frills and frivolities of *My Fair Lady*, which elaborated even further in the direction of romance and became the most successful stage musical of its era.

On stage, *My Fair Lady* attempted effects that were cinematic in intention and result: scrim curtains and back lighting acted like lap-dissolves, and a pin of light on a performer's face achieved the intimacy of a close-up. Ironically, but maybe inevitably, the film version (1964) seems more stately and stolid behind the patina of success. It does retain Rex Harrison and Stanley Holloway from the original Broadway show, as well as Cecil Beaton, who designed costumes and supervised the production design, and whose contributions are a mixed blessing. But the original has not been preserved intact; the lily has been self-indulgently gilded, and it needs air.

The decision to retain what seems to be the work's indispensable theatricality does not necessarily upset one's expectations. Some of Cukor's films (*Adam's Rib*, *Edward My Son*, even *Romeo and Juliet*) contained theatrical prologues, and proceeded from that premise to manifest their cinematic essence. There is a tension established between stage and cinema in some of his best work, and one of the major pleasures in *My Fair Lady* resides in the way it occasionally reminds the audience of the hallowed origins of the film, as when pedestrians freeze in their tracks, group after group, until the speckless, overlit Covent Garden set is full and resumes movement. Or in the way Cukor plays with our expectations of theatricality and then mischievously upsets them, for instance, by having real horses race in the foreground of the stylized Ascot Gavotte number. A frozen Freddy Eynsford-Hill, between banks of flowers, stranded on Wimpole Street until the next number comes along, simply tells us that the character can only exist within the boundaries of the stage, that to deny its theatricality is to deny it life.

The contrast between the two styles is further pursued (as much as Beaton's production design will allow) to establish the two worlds which form its background. Edwardian society is portrayed in highly formalized poses, cool greys and whites; suffocating in Beaton's attar of roses, they uphold the most theatrical elements of the play. The low life of costermongers, pub patrons and flower vendors is in richer browns and reds. A lovely *leitmotif* of flowers links the absurdly exquisite creatures in their finery and their plumes to the earth-coloured liveliness of Covent Garden. The staging of the musical numbers, the music itself, take their stylistic cues from class distinctions: recitatives and ballads for the upper classes that sound operetta-ish and mid-brow (the most conservative of these, 'On the street where you live', belongs appropriately to the pale juvenile lead); and rowdy routines for Holloway and his cronies, intricately choreographed and photographed, reeking of life and the music-hall. Between the lifeless but beautiful and the lively but grotesque lies

116

My Fair Lady: Rex Harrison, Audrey Hepburn

Eliza's choice, and logically her songs range from the spiteful 'Just You Wait' to the rapturous 'I Could Have Danced All Night'.

Hamstrung from all sides by the play's success and by the sheer opulence of the undertaking, Cukor has reserved for himself the film's only controversial choice, Audrey Hepburn's Eliza. Overcoming the strait-lacing of the Beaton gowns and the unlikelihood of a singing voice that seems too obviously a playback, she achieves a special radiance that owes nothing to the theatre and belongs somewhere between movies and fairytale. (The picture bypasses the play in its Cinderella references: a clock strikes as Higgins changes his mind and enigmatically drops his change into Eliza's basket, launching her into her new life; Eliza frantically looks for the ring that Higgins has hurled into the ashes.) After Higgins' speech about the grandeur of the English language, concluding with '... and

117

conquer you will' (a speech which Harrison delivers with a fervour hitherto absent from a performance honed by a thousand representations), Cukor cuts to Hepburn, intelligence awakening in the inquisitive doe eyes, the pinched little prude from the slums suddenly glowing with awareness and passion.

At its best, the filmed *My Fair Lady* demonstrates that Shaw can do very well without all the Lerner and Loew embellishments. The after-the-ball confrontation between Eliza and Higgins, when they allow themselves for the first time the luxury of baring their feelings to each other, she berating him for his lofty disregard for her humanity, he striking back at her calculated taunt that she must not be allowed to keep his ring, is transposed almost intact from the original Shaw, and calls neither for music nor the conventions of the musical comedy. The director's response to the material is also visible in the film's other highlight, again a non-musical scene, and one that recalls similar situations in other Cukor films. Standing on the stairway, above her sponsors, dressed for the ball where she will get to dance with a prince, silent, tremulous with fear and anticipation, Eliza shares her fragile obsession with other Cukor heroines from Mary Evans on; who, in a splendid moment of illumination, discover a certain greatness in themselves.

8: Postscript

My Fair Lady became Cukor's most honoured and financially successful film, and his subsequent work has been largely dealt with as a sort of postscript to a distinguished career. One of these projects, it's true, was hampered by circumstances that made it less than ideal. In *Justine* (1969), the director was asked by producer Pandro S. Berman, with whom he had worked on *Sylvia Scarlett* and *Bhowani Junction*, to take over from Joseph Strick. Cukor inherited a motley cast and a script which, despite last-minute revisions, failed to satisfy those connected with the project. As usual in these cases, the film had to contend with the literary reputation of the original novel or novels, for the adaptation borrowed incidents from all four parts of *The Alexandria Quartet*. Cukor was perfunctorily credited with his usual finesse in handling performers and the picture was dismissed; the reason was that, no longer relying on the star and script guidelines that characterized his work up to the mid-Fifties, Cukor had confirmed his position as one of Hollywood's visual stylists, and this without renouncing his themes. It is easier to do justice, especially in the limited space of a review, to dialogue and characterization than to the rhythms and felicities of a visual style hinted at in *The Chapman Report* and *Heller in Pink Tights*.

Justine was not the first film on which Cukor had replaced another director in mid-filming. In 1959, when Charles Vidor died shortly after beginning *Song Without End*, Cukor was called in to complete the picture, most of which shows his style, along with a lack of involvement with the main character. And yet, Franz Liszt, that most theatrical of musicians, would appear to be an ideal subject, with his penchant for staging his own public appearances, the ham actor upstaging the virtuoso. *Song Without End* does relish the spectacle of Dirk Bogarde removing his gloves and dropping them on the stage before taking his place at the keyboard, or signalling with a snap of the famous fingers that he is ready to take a bow from his hotel window. The private vagaries of Liszt are of much less interest to Cukor who, naturally, ends up by making a case for both of his mistresses. Nevertheless, *Justine* is not merely an inherited project: within the limits of one feature, and one hardly as long as Cukor originally envisioned, there is enough Durrell in it to satisfy the literary-minded (and little of his purple prose, mercifully), but there is also a lot of Cukor. A dialogue exchange from the first of the novels offers a clue to involvement. 'What is happening to Nessim?' demands Darley the narrator, to which Justine replies, 'I no longer know. When there is something to hide, one becomes an actor. It forces all the people round one to act as well.'

Durrell's all-purpose metaphor was the city of Alexandria. His prose evocation of the Middle East carries memories and notions of other European writers who, since Pierre Louys on, have made the Orient a surrogate for the Forbidden. On the screen, *Justine* refers the viewer to his memory of films like *Morocco* and *Casablanca*, a perfect equivalence. Bazaars and cafés, hovels and palaces are re-created within the Hollywood sound stages, with only a few leftover location shots jarring the deliberately artificial mood. Within this closed space, metaphors proliferate, some sexual, some political. Transvestism runs rampant: male kooch dancers back Melissa in her cabaret act, Pombal dons the costume of an odalisque, Toto fatally impersonates Justine, the British ambassador arrives in full regalia at the masked ball, another actor setting up his performance in the vast masquerade of the city.

Every character, with the exception of Melissa (Anna Karina), who is exactly what she seems, is caught in a web of deception. And the film makes her the privileged character rather than the tiresomely enigmatic Justine (Anouk Aimée). (This is the first sign of subversion in a film that constantly upsets our expectations of the genre.) It is Melissa who, though unawares, holds the thread to the maze, whose function is to make the other characters see the truth, all the more pivotal a role since plot incident consistently offers more than one explanation. For instance, the sense of foreboding that overcomes

120

Masquerade: Michael York, Anouk Aimée, John Vernon in *Justine*

Justine and Darley (Michael York) as they realize that their love-
making has been spied on, a suspicion that is soon confirmed; only
later do we discover that we have been misled by the cliché-like
situation. Likewise, the camera steals up to Justine and Nessim (John
Vernon) at the very moment when words lose their exact significance.
It would have been folly to attempt to preserve the quadruple viewpoint of the novels; nevertheless, what *Les Girls* attempted within a
comedy context is not too removed from what *Justine* does in
dramatic terms.

The temptation is there to read *Justine* as we once read
Casablanca, and the new film could be construed as an affectionate
homage to old-style Hollywood movie-making, were it not for the
fact that Cukor has deftly and deliberately subverted the signs so that
they lead no more to hopeful heroics and honourable solutions, but
to death and disenchantment. In this existential roundelay, Cohen
(Jack Albertson) will die grasping Melissa's perfume flask, Narouz
(Robert Forster) will be sacrificed by his own people, Pursewarden
(Dirk Bogarde) will take his own life having realized that the grand
romantic intrigue was nothing but a banal political ploy. Durrell

121

Travels with my Aunt: Maggie Smith as Aunt Augusta

intended his characters to be haunted by the lingering presence of lovers past; perhaps Cukor's ultimate metaphor was to have *Justine* attended by the ghosts of von Sternberg, Curtiz *et al*. In any case, his film attests to the resilience and elasticity of the traditional Hollywood modes.

Film has helped to perpetuate the misconceptions and prejudices under which the elderly must live, purportedly adult films usually exploiting the subject of old age either for ready-made pathos or facile sociology. Two of Cukor's recent films approach their venerable heroes and heroines with the less than reverential aspect of a contemporary, and their dreams and delusions with gallant humour and understanding. In *Travels with my Aunt* (1972) and *Love among the Ruins* (1975) Cukor – now, along with Alfred Hitchcock, the American cinema's oldest working director – supports the conviction that no one is ever too old to renounce desire or desirability, that such needs are indeed integral to being human, and are therefore for ever.

It is quite possible to admire *Travels with my Aunt* while retaining a few misgivings about the presence of Maggie Smith in a title role destined at some stage of the negotiations for Katharine Hepburn. That such problematic casting means disaster to a picture is a comfortable theory to which most critics and film-makers – once, even Cukor – have fervently subscribed; yet one need only recall the prodigious feats of, among others, Hitchcock, Renoir and Ophuls when constrained by less than ideal performers, to realize that *Travels with my Aunt* need not be better or worse for lacking Hepburn, only different. Ms Smith manages the flashbacks as Hepburn never could – the subsequent *Love among the Ruins* confirms this – so one should be thankful for at least one searing transition from (real) youth to (bogus) old age, from ecstasy to ecstasy remembered, which Ms Smith pulls off to perfection.

Also predictable, at least from Anglo-Saxon critics, was a reaction of dismay at still another Graham Greene novel being served up as film fodder; only this time the book is not Greene's most serious but rather a playful parody of such literary lights as Eric Ambler (and Greene himself) who often wander these haunts. The picture tells its own story, loosely adapted by Jay Presson Allen and Hugh Wheeler; the cinematic equivalent of the Greene pastiches become stylish flashbacks in the style of Colette, Labiche and Noël Coward. Both film and novel, like their deceptively old-fashioned heroine, accommodate wisdom and tomfoolery. The basic difference resides in the fact that, whereas Greene filtered the picaresque events of the tale through his Catholic misogyny, Cukor's Aunt Augusta becomes living proof of Ashley Montagu's dictum that 'it's the function of women to teach men how to be human'.

Looking and behaving like a cross between a benign witch and a decrepit cocotte, Augusta Bertram descends upon her middle-aged nephew Henry Pulling (Alec McCowen), whose life has hitherto run on a timetable as sterile and precise as that of the commuter trains that every so often puff past his flowerbeds, and inveigles him into a shady scheme which takes them to Paris, Istanbul, the high seas and finally to a deserted stretch of the North African coast. Along the way, Henry loses his virginity to a hippie girl (Cindy Williams), under the joint influence of Aunt Augusta and marihuana. Augusta, Henry deduces from her reminiscing, has loved not wisely but well and almost continuously; her commitment to life is summed up in a *cri de coeur*, 'I have looked the world in the eye and I've never despised anyone. Love nothing, lose nothing.'

By the film's end, Henry has come to see life more deeply and more clearly; he has realized, for instance, that to live is to be corrupted by life, and that despite some exquisite debauchery Aunt Augusta has preserved intact her youthful dreams and illusions, most of which centre on Mr Visconti (Robert Stephens), the rake who swept her off her willing feet at the Gare de Lyon more than half a century before. The film literally confirms Augusta as the life-giving force. The final revelation, playfully hinted at all along, is that she is in reality Henry's mother, and that he is one of her several children by Mr Visconti. He, the embodiment of English middle-class propriety, a bastard and half-Italian to boot! It's a mind-boggling revelation that sends Henry into an Italianate paroxysm, flapping his arms wildly and declaiming, 'Mamma mia, Mamma mia!'

The Augusta/Henry relationship, and the tension between her guilt-free Continental pragmatism and his rigid British morality, is developed throughout in a playfully realistic style. Nevertheless, pending the release of *The Bluebird*, this remains Cukor at his most fantastic, and many scenes stress the demiurgical qualities of Aunt Augusta. Like a true spirit, she is capable of assuming different forms: schoolgirl (in Paris during *la belle époque*), prostitute (in a Venetian bordello in the Twenties), kept woman (again in Paris at some indeterminate period), and ultimately a grotesque crone, the final irreversible mask imposed by life itself. All these images coalesce in the face of Aunt Augusta, as we join the camera in refusing the imposture of old age. At her conjuring, resources seem to materialize in the form of old admirers, illegitimate offspring, improbable gallantries that she never bothers to explain, as when the Turkish chief of police allows her to go free after catching her red-handed in the act of smuggling money into the country.

The reversal of roles is the most definitive in a Cukor film, for not only must Augusta cut Henry's umbilical cord (figuratively, of course: at the prospect of their impromptu trip to the Continent, Henry clings to his garden shears), but he must learn from her his name, lineage and true nature, at the end matching wits with his own unsuspecting father, Mr Visconti, and beating him at his own confidence game. If we are to trust the laws of heredity, we know beforehand the outcome as the coin which supposedly will decide Henry's future spins in mid-air, and the final image freezes.

Love among the Ruins: Richard Pearson, Laurence Olivier, Katharine Hepburn

Love among the Ruins also deals with the incongruity of passion in late middle age, drawing its comic and dramatic insights from the small social deceits that make up a time and a place, in this case Edwardian London. Written by James Costigan as a vehicle for Alfred Lunt and Lynn Fontanne, subsequently adapted for television and the personalities of Katharine Hepburn and Laurence Olivier, the film complies with the requirements of the medium in its uncluttered visuals and an acting style that seems to compensate for the pettiness of the video screen. Other than that, there are few close-ups, the takes are as long as one would expect from Cukor, and the camera moves with fluid elegance while still keeping a respectful distance from these formidable fools.

The period is that of *My Fair Lady*, the terrain that of *Adam's Rib*. Jessica Medlicott, a dowager, is sued by an impecunious young man for breach of promise; she seeks the legal assistance of Sir Arthur Granville-Jones, one of London's most illustrious barristers and her contemporary, who cherishes after half a century the memory of his short affair with the lady, at the time when she was a touring soubrette and he a dashing law student. Meeting a lifetime after, he is bitterly disappointed when she fails to remember their liaison and foolishly jealous when Jessica makes it clear to him that she is still quite capable not merely of entertaining passion but of consummating it. To win the case, but also to heal his wounded ego, Granville-Jones decides to pass Jessica off to the jury as a pathetic old woman duped by a young arrivist into a promise of marriage she will hardly live to keep. Told to appear in court in her widow's weeds, she turns out in her most resplendent finery; when he hints that she is well past passion, she raises such a rumpus that she has to be forcefully dragged from court. Granville-Jones wins the case at the expense of Jessica's dignity and self-respect. In a final twist that should not come as much of a surprise to anyone who knows Cukor, she admits to remembering their youthful fling in detail. So as not to encourage any sentimentality on his part, which would have been fatal to the case, she chose instead to drive him to outrage. To him, as to his peers, what would be considered permissible, even admirable, in a man of a certain age would seem inadmissible in a woman. Jessica, the crafty old trouper, has offered herself as a fool, while master-minding her defence all along.

In short, this is 1911 and a woman must resort to such duplicities to gain absolution from the world. Yet the taste is of irony, not of ashes, as the once and future lovers exit arm in arm into the glorious English summer. The effect is neither final nor elegiac; this is a director revisiting the conventions and sensibilities of younger days, and in the process bringing off a superb coup as matchmaker. Nothing seems too silly or too undignified to these grandly theatrical people. Olivier, in particular, is unique at rendering various conflicting moods with a heavenly roll of the eyes, or by raising and dropping his voice a full octave in mid-sentence. In the reading of one single line, for instance, 'She doesn't – remember – me!', he crams the anxiety of first love and the exasperation of old age. Whether in tears or in outrage, Hepburn improves a script which, for all its custom tailoring, is watery Shaw, spiced-up Barrie and full-flavoured Rattigan. As the actress and the barrister pitch impersonations against each other, Cukor encourages them to 'perform' rather than to 'be'. Ultimately, incongruously, this television film is about the theatre. The director has come full circle. All the stories, all the legends and backstage tales about Hepburn, Olivier and Cukor end in a smile of complicity which the picture offers as a curtain call.

126

Filmography

George Cukor

Born 7 July 1899 in New York.
Educated at the De Witt Clinton High School.
Entered the theatre in 1918 as stage manager. Directed plays in Rochester NY and New York City. Went to Hollywood in 1929.

Mr Cukor's comments are culled from interviews taped at his home in Hollywood in December 1968 and April 1969. The author's clarifications appear in brackets and are marked Ed.

A. Credited work

1. FILMS AS DIALOGUE DIRECTOR

River of Romance (1929)

Production Company	Paramount
Director	Richard Wallace
Script	Ethel Doherty. Based on the play *Magnolia* by Booth Tarkington
Dialogue	Dan Totheroh, John Weaver
Dialogue Director	George Cukor

With Buddy Rogers, Henry B. Walthall, Mary Brian, June Collyer, Wallace Beery.

Released in USA, July 1929. Running time, 80 min.
Distributor: Paramount.

CUKOR: I didn't watch many films before I came to Hollywood. When I was very young in New York, I was infatuated with the stage and had a very snobbish attitude towards movies. If you had told me then that I was going to go into them and settle in California, I would have laughed. But, as a child, I used to watch them. I saw the Max Linder comedies, for instance. Therefore, the streets of Paris were familiar to me at a very early age. As a young man, I was interested in certain pictures. I saw *Way Down East* and was very much impressed, more so than by the Limehouse story, *Broken Blossoms*. Even then, I thought of Griffith as a kind of genius. At times his films may seem *démodé*, out of fashion, but a hundred years from now, if they are still shown, people will realize that feeling transcends fashion, they'll see how strong and clear they are.

127

In '29, I left the theatre. I had done by then quite a bit of work on the stage, both in Rochester and in New York. But things were very difficult there, just like they are now. Although the stage had a great many stars – always a very important element of American life – even *they* were no guarantee of success. Even with a good play, you didn't always succeed. It had become rather a chancy business. While all the talkies seemed to succeed. And a lot of stage people went West. Hollywood had no more use for title writers; instead they needed dialogue directors. My first job as such was at Paramount, in a film called *River of Romance*, directed by Richard Wallace. I never directed the play from which it derived but I knew it fairly well. It was *Magnolia* by Booth Tarkington, a play of a first-rate literary quality. It was from an idea that Lionel Barrymore gave Tarkington, a satire of the gallantry of the Old South, about how a truly courageous man is but an illusion. And dealing with Southern aristocrats, who were rather illiterate, it depended on a brilliant approximation of Southern speech.

So, there was this distinguished text but they would have nothing to do with it. They were making so much money that anything they would put in the actors' mouths worked. They had no idea what working from the text meant, or of what I was trying to do. So they cut most of the funny dialogue and retained what they considered the entertaining parts.

I never gave up entirely the idea of returning to the theatre. In the Thirties, Katharine Hepburn wanted me to direct her stage come-back (*Jane Eyre*, Ed). And Gilbert Miller, once my associate on Broadway, wanted me to direct Audrey Hepburn in the adaptation of *Gigi*, around '51. I returned to the stage once, in the summer of 1955: I directed *The Chalk Garden* for Irene Selznick, up to the Boston opening. Then Metro needed me back for additional cutting on *Bhowani Junction* and another director, Albert Marre, brought the play to Broadway.

All Quiet on the Western Front (1930)

Production Company	Universal
Producer	Carl Laemmle, Jr
Director	Lewis Milestone
Script	Maxwell Anderson
Adaptation	George Abbott. Based on the novel by Erich Maria Remarque
Dialogue Director	George Cukor

With Louis Wolheim, Lewis Ayres, John Wray, Raymond Griffith.

Released in USA, April 1930. Running time, 152 min.
Distributor: Universal.

CUKOR: It was at Paramount that I met David O. Selznick, then Executive Assistant to B. P. Schulberg and also General Manager of the West Coast Studios. His brother Myron became my manager. David introduced me to Lewis Milestone, who was getting ready to start *All Quiet on the Western Front* for Universal. Maxwell

Anderson was writing the scenario and I had directed one of his plays, *Gypsy*, the year before. It was, as a matter of fact, my last Broadway play. So, we worked together on the dialogue and, at the same time, I tested the actors. I must say that the vitality and strength of that picture are all Milestone's. What I did was work very hard on individual scenes. I already had some sort of reputation in getting results from inexperienced performers.

Recently Fred Zinnemann sent me a snapshot of himself as an extra in the picture. He was then a very young boy, freshly arrived in Hollywood to study American production methods.

One Hour With You (1932)

Production Company	Paramount
Producer	Ernst Lubitsch
Director	Ernst Lubitsch
Script	Samson Raphaelson. Based on the play *Nur ein Traum* by Lothar Schmidt
Dialogue Director	George Cukor

With Maurice Chevalier, Jeanette MacDonald, Genevieve Tobin, Charlie Ruggles. Released in USA, March 1932. Running time, 80 min. Distributor: Paramount.

CUKOR: Everybody is interested in the trip-ups. Lubitsch, who had done all these very successful, very clever pictures with Jeanette MacDonald and Maurice Chevalier, was busy doing a serious story, *The Man I Killed*. Schulberg assigned me to direct *One Hour With You*, a Lubitsch production, under Lubitsch's supervision. It was very early in the game, and I did the best I could but it really wasn't very good. Or at least, it wasn't what they really wanted, which was a Lubitsch picture and only Lubitsch could make them. They were not happy with what I had done but they kept saying: Stick with it. Then Lubitsch finished the other picture and took over, reshooting practically the whole film. I may have shot some of what you see in the film; also there was a French version being made at the same time. All I remember is I behaved extremely well in this awkward situation. Schulberg was rather a tough man: he decided to take my name off the picture and I sued Paramount. I don't think I won, but my name stayed in the credits.

By now, Selznick had gone to RKO and I wanted to follow but Paramount would not allow me to, some internal thing, dreary studio politics. But, as part of the settlement of my suit, I was permitted to leave. RKO took over part of my contract so that I was still being paid the Paramount scales. When I finally went to Metro, I realized I had been working all these years at a very modest salary. Then I had to wage some kind of revolution.

One Hour With You is really a Lubitsch picture and if you think you can detect what I did in it, you're imagining things. Lubitsch's pictures were brilliant, even if they lacked feeling. And yet, *The Patriot* was very impressive and moving. I don't remember the German ones with Pola Negri but I remember being aware of their special power. He changed his style when he came over and had a big success with the American pictures which were very witty and wonderfully constructed. He did a couple of serious pictures in Hollywood but they were sentimental and had none of the power. I think the reason is that it's very difficult to work in a foreign language, to learn the nuances. He could be very witty on that very subject. He told me that when they began to make German-speaking versions in America, at the Brooklyn Studios, they tried to synch Murnau's *Faust*. Jannings played Mephisto and a very pretty girl who was under contract, Camilla Horn, had played the classical part of Marguerite. But she could not do the voice as she had *a drug-store accent*! A little, if I may say so, like the current Juliets. So, you see, he was very aware of this in German. However, in his American pictures, if an actor had a certain quality that he liked, he employed him regardless of voice or accent. For instance, if he wanted to portray a king as an old comfortable bourgeois, he would get George Barbier, who had the right visual quality but who spoke with a mid-Western accent that had no style, no distinction and it spoiled the illusion. Part of the style comes from speech. Even in English; if I had to work in England, with English actors, I'm afraid some of the finer points would be lost to me.

Well, this happened to Lubitsch in his serious work here. He didn't want his comedies to have any feeling. Now, my idea of comedy is that they should always touch you unexpectedly. At least, that's the way I've made them. For this, you need modern virtuoso performances: Judy Holliday, who had the knack to catch you in the throat when you least expected it. Or Ruth Gordon in *The Matchmaker*, playing it broad and suddenly you found yourself involved. There was a wonderful actress named Laurette Taylor. I did two plays with her, and in one, *The Cardboard Lover*, she was light as a feather until you found yourself moved to tears. Réjane must have had that quality; very few nowadays have it. But Lubitsch never constructed his pictures to get you involved, he didn't want to. He was a most accomplished man. But our views on style and comedy were different.

2. FILMS AS DIRECTOR

Grumpy (1930)

Production Company	Paramount
Directors	George Cukor, Cyril Gardner
Script	Doris Anderson. Based on the play by Horace Hodges and Thomas Wigney Percyval
Director of Photography	David Abel
Sound	Harold C. Lewis

Cyril Maude (*'Grumpy' Bullivant*), Phillips Holmes (*Ernest Heron*), Paul Cavanaugh (*Jarvis*), Francis Dade (*Virginia*), Halliwell Hobbes (*Ruddock*), Doris Luray (*Susan*), Olaf Hytten (*Keble*), Paul Lukas (*Berci*), Robert Bolder (*Merridew*), Colin Kenny (*Dawson*).

Released in USA, August 1930; GB, August 1931. Running time, 74 min. Distributor: Paramount.

130

CUKOR: Cyril Gardner, my co-director, had been a cutter and film-cutters were now in a peculiar, anomalous position. In silent days, directors used to consult them. Sometimes they were writers and the director could bounce ideas off them and that's how stories were written. Gardner was a very intelligent fellow, a kind of No-Man; he knew what could be done and what was impossible or impractical. He was very nice to me, I learnt a lot from him. We were assigned my first picture, together, an adaptation of a stage success. An old English actor named Cyril Maude, who had played the role 1,500 times, was signed to do it. It was a trifle about a lovable, ill-tempered lawyer who was something of a detective. Very old-fashioned stuff, at least for the stage.

The Virtuous Sin (1930)

Production Company	Paramount
Directors	George Cukor, Louis Gasnier
Script	Martin Brown, Louise Long. Based on the play *The General* by Lajos Zilahy
Director of Photography	David Abel
Editor	Otho Lovering
Sound	Harold M. McNiff

Walter Huston (*General Gregori Platoff*), Kay Francis (*Maria Ivanovna*), Kenneth MacKenna (*Lt Victor Sablin*), Jobyna Howland (*Alexandra Stroganov*), Paul Cavanaugh (*Capt Orloff*), Eric Kalkhurst (*Lt Glinka*), Oscar Apfel (*Major Ivanoff*), Gordon McLeod (*Col Nikitin*), Youcca Troubetzkoy (*Capt Sobakin*), Victor Potel (*Sentry*), Bud Fine (*Orderly*), Lew Meehan (*Jailer*), Hal Price (*Soldier*), Ann Brody (*Anna*).

Released in USA, October 1930; GB, June 1931. Running time, 80 min.
Distributor: Paramount.
GB title: *Cast Iron*

CUKOR: *The Virtuous Sin* was a ghastly picture. My co-director, Louis Gasnier, was a well known, very experienced French director who had been in the business for years but still spoke with a tremendous French accent. The story came from a very bad Hungarian play, a stupid story – Huston and Kay Francis were ridiculous in it. Jobyna Howland, a friend of mine and a very funny woman, played the madam of a brothel, or 'cabaret' as it was called in the dialogue. She came from the stage, had a very interesting personality and a way with lines. She became famous in pictures in one single scene. She was playing a scene with a child performer by the name of Mitzi Green (in *Honey*, Ed), a smart-alecky brat who keeps saying, 'I've got a secret, I've got a secret,' and asking for money. She finally gets Jobyna to give it to her, and then she tells her secret, which of course turns out to be absolutely nothing. And Jobyna, who was a strong woman, picks up the brat and throws her clear across the room. It was so boldly done that I stole the scene many years later. I don't know if you saw the complete *A Star is Born*, but there was a scene when a mother pesters James Mason to let himself be photographed with her child, and Mason picks up the child and throws her out of the set. It was very funny.

The Royal Family of Broadway (1930)

Production Company	Paramount
Directors	George Cukor, Cyril Gardner
Script	Herman Mankiewicz, Gertrude Purcell. Based on the play *The Royal Family* by Edna Ferber and George S. Kaufman
Director of Photography	George Folsey
Editor	Edward Dmytryk
Musical Director	Jay Gorney
Sound	C. A. Tuthill

Ina Claire (*Julia Cavendish*), Fredric March (*Tony Cavendish*), Henrietta Crosman (*Fanny Cavendish*), Mary Brian (*Gwen Cavendish*), Charles Starrett (*Perry Stewart*), Arnold Korff (*Oscar Wolfe*), Frank Conroy (*Gilbert Marshall*), Royal G. Stout (*Joe*), Elsie Edmond (*Della*), Murray Alper (*McDermott*), Wesley Stark (*Hall Boy*), Herschel Mayall (*Doctor*).

Released in USA, December 1930; GB, November 1931. Running time, 82 min. Distributor: Paramount.

CUKOR: I was supposed to direct the play *The Royal Family* for Jed Harris in New York in 1928. I never did, but I knew the play rather well and the Barrymores were good friends of mine. I had directed Ethel in *The Constant Wife*. I didn't know John very well in those days – we hadn't worked together yet. Ina Claire was supposed to be Ethel, although there was no resemblance at all between the two. And the mother was supposed to stand for Ethel's grandmother, a fact that always infuriated Ethel as she had been a distinguished woman and the character was distorted in the play. The Barrymores hated the play, but I found it very funny, very cleverly written by Kaufman. It wasn't supposed to be real or serious.

By then I was feeling my way in pictures. My cameraman was George Folsey, and we had this idea to follow March on his way to take a bath, up the stairs and through several rooms, as he strips merrily along, in one take. It was very difficult as everything had to be pushed out of the way by hand to make way for the enormous camera crane. I was very proud of it.

Curiously enough, the picture was not a great popular success. People said it was too sophisticated for movie audiences. They even dropped the last part of the title, so that it became simply *The Royal Family*, after it opened in New York. Maybe it was Ina Claire. She never became a movie star. When she started her film career, she was already in her thirties. It was too late. She had been very pretty and appeared in the Ziegfeld Follies, later working for Belasco. She had slowly acquired a lot of subtlety and elegance, and she became a great star on Broadway playing sympathetic heroines. She was a rare thing but she had no movie personality, she didn't come across.

Tarnished Lady (1931)

Production Company	Paramount
Producer	Walter Wanger
Director	George Cukor
Script	Donald Ogden Stewart, Based on his story *New York Lady*
Director of Photography	Larry Williams
Editor	Barney Rogan
Song: 'I'm Yours'	John W. Green, E. Y. Harburg
Sound	Harold Fingerlin

Tallulah Bankhead (*Nancy Courtney*), Clive Brook (*Norman Cravath*), Phoebe Foster (*Germaine Prentiss*), Alexander Kirkland (*DeWitt Taylor*), Osgood Perkins (*Ben Sterner*), Elizabeth Patterson (*Mrs Courtney*), Eric Blore (*Jeweller*), Berton Churchill (*Tom*), Dewey Robinson (*Tony*), Ed Gargan (*Al*), Cora Witherspoon (*Miss Gifford*).

Released in USA, April 1931; GB, January 1932. Running time, 80 min. Distributor: Paramount.

CUKOR: *The Royal Family* was made at the Paramount studios in Long Island. While I was at work there, Walter Wanger approached me to direct a story called *New York Lady* by Donald Ogden Stewart. Don was a very witty, very humorous writer and we were to make more pictures together. *Tarnished Lady*, as the picture came to be called, was the talkie debut of Tallulah Bankhead, fresh from her London triumph, and she sounded *too* British for words. She didn't look too good either. Maybe if we had made the picture in California, it would have turned out better. It got very bad reviews. And for many years afterwards I worked exclusively in Hollywood.

Girls About Town (1931)

Production Company	Paramount
Director	George Cukor
Script	Raymond Griffith, Brian Marlow. Based on a story by Zoë Akins
Director of Photography	Ernest Haller

Kay Francis (*Wanda Howard*), Joel McCrea (*Jim Baker*), Lilyan Tashman (*Marie Bailey*), Eugene Pallette (*Benjamin Thomas*), Allan Dinehart (*Jerry Chafe*), Lucille

Cukor and company on *Girls about Town*

Webster (*Mrs Benjamin Thomas*), Anderson Lawler (*Alex Howard*), Lucille Brown (*Edna*), George Barbier (*Webster*), Robert McWade (*Simms*), Louise Beavers (*Hattie*), Judith Wood (*Winnie*), Adrienne Ames (*Anne*), Claire Dodd (*Dot*), Hazel Howard (*Joy*), Patricia Caron (*Billie*), Katherine DeMille.

Released in USA, October 1931. Running time, 66 min.
Distributor: Paramount.

CUKOR: This was the period of the gold-digger or playgirl, in reality whores who charged $500 an evening or $1,000 a weekend. All very brittle, the sets very *moderne*. Zoë Akins wrote these parts to perfection, the dangerous good-hearted playgirl. There was one here for Lilyan Tashman, an adorable funny girl with a cat-like face. She was rarely good in pictures, but here, since the part was written for her, she appeared terribly relaxed.

In those days at Paramount I used to watch other directors at work, but not too much. It wasn't – or isn't – *de rigueur* to watch others at work. For one thing, you can't learn much about a man's work if you just stand there, on the set, for a short

134

while. You must spend a great deal of time so that you can see cause and effect, how a scene evolves. I don't say I wasn't interested, but I was not the way some people are with movies. I wasn't absorbed the way I had been about the theatre, in my younger days.

What Price Hollywood? (1932)

Production Company	RKO
Producer	David O. Selznick
Associate Producer	Pandro S. Berman
Director	George Cukor
Script	Gene Fowler, Rowland Brown. Based on a story by Adela Rogers St John Hyland
Dialogue	Jane Murfin, Ben Markson
Director of Photography	Charles Rosher
Editor	Jack Kitchin
Montage Sequences	Slavko Vorkapich
Set Decorator	Carroll Clark
Music	Max Steiner
Sound	George Ellis

Constance Bennett (*Mary Evans*), Lowell Sherman (*Maximilian Carey*), Neil Hamilton (*Lonny Borden*), Gregory Ratoff (*Julius Saxe*), Brooks Benedict (*Muto*), Louise Beavers (*Bonita*), Eddie Anderson (*James*), Florence Roberts (*Diner*), Nick Caruso (*Cook*), Bryant Washburn (*Washed-up Star*), Gordon De Main (*Yes Man*), Heinie Conklin (*Car Owner*), Eddie Dunn (*Doorman at Grauman's Chinese Theatre*), Phil Tead (*Jimmy*), Wilfred Lucas (*Bill*), Eric Wilton (*Mary's Butler*), James Mason (*Roberts*), Josephine Whittell (*Miss Dupont*).

Released in USA, June 1932; GB, November 1932. Running time, 88 min. Distributor: RKO Pathé.

CUKOR: Selznick had left Paramount on rather unpleasant terms. He was very young and yet he had been offered this fabulous job, to head RKO, and since we had worked together, he requested that I go with him. After my suit, I followed him there. Selznick loved Hollywood, he wasn't at all cynical about it, and he wanted to make a film about it. That's how *What Price Hollywood?* came to be made. It was a rather amusing idea cooked up by Adela Rogers St John and other writers who knew the Hollywood scene well. It was satirical but only in part. The director in the picture was a composite of several. Maybe Marshall Neilan, or William Desmond Taylor. Casting was very important: Lowell Sherman, who played the role very interestingly, was a sardonic, polished performer; maybe not an actor of the first class but damn well near. He was not a classical type like John Barrymore, for he had a slightly unpleasant face: you remember him as the villain of *Way Down East*. He was a star by New York standards. And now, he was cast so right! He played an arrogant, difficult director, sweet to the girl but mean to everybody else. But it was so arranged that all these qualities which kept Sherman from being a top star worked in his behalf here. He became sympathetic, so that you actually felt sorry for him and his death scene was agonizing. *What Price Hollywood?* was the one picture about Hollywood that had any feeling, up to that time.

A Star is Born is more or less a remake. But it was totally rewritten. The director became an actor. Actually, there was an actor, the husband of Marguerite de la Motte I think, who killed himself in the same way, walking off the beach in Malibu or Santa Monica (John Bowers, Ed). I didn't direct it then, as I was under contract to Metro and about to do *Camille*. But both Selznick and William Wellman, who was to direct, were very close friends. I remember I went to visit John Barrymore at the time with a script that I thought would be good for him. Jack was drying out in some sort of rest home, a private institution in Culver City. I had made several pictures with him by then and he never drank while he was working in them. He was a most attractive man, enormously cultivated and very vulnerable. He had the reputation of being difficult to work with but I always found him charming. And now he was living in this abandoned, sordid boarding-house, and had a male attendant called Kelly. We sat in a small room next to the dining-room where all the tables were laid for early dinner and I must have looked uneasy, for he said rather humorously: 'Don't worry, it's not dangerous. This is not an asylum and no lunatic is going to come through here pretending to be Napoleon.' I was very impressed and told Selznick and Wellman about my visit. They wrote the scene into the screenplay, and many years later I found myself directing that scene when I remade *A Star is Born*.

A Bill of Divorcement (1932)

Production Company	RKO Radio
Producer	David O. Selznick
Director	George Cukor
Assistant Director	Dewey Starkey
Script	Howard Estabrook, Harry Wagstaff Gribble. Based on the play by Clemence Dane
Director of Photography	Sid Hickox
Editor	Arthur Roberts
Set Designer	Carroll Clark
Costumes	Josette De Lima
Music	Max Steiner
Piano Concerto	W. Franke Harling
Sound	George Ellis

John Barrymore (*Hilary*), Billie Burke (*Margaret*), Katharine Hepburn (*Sydney*), David Manners (*Kit*), Henry Stephenson (*Dr Alliot*), Paul Cavanaugh (*Gray Meredith*), Elizabeth Patterson (*Aunt Hester*), Gayle Evers (*Bassett*), Dennis O'Keefe (*Dancing Extra*).

Released in USA, September 1932; GB, April 1933. Running time, 70 min. Distributor: RKO Radio.

CUKOR: It was Katharine Hepburn's first picture. We were to make seven more together although, at the time, I was inclined to doubt it. She was terribly opinionated, usually about things she knew nothing or little of. I told her then that I couldn't take her seriously. But from the moment she played her first scene, she was at home. She had no self-consciousness at all, she was born for the movies although she didn't know it, coming as she did from the stage. She looked at Barrymore, who was playing her father, with adoration. And she wept. Jack and I looked at each other; we couldn't believe it as we had only seen the screen test she had made. I'll tell you more about that test later. Jack was very sweet to her. He made a slight pass at her, felt it wasn't going to work and became an absolute angel to the girl. In their scenes together, he would always try to favour her. Kate was a success, of course, and she never forgot Barrymore's kindness.

Then, many years later, Darryl Zanuck wanted to film an Emlyn Williams play, *Light of Heart*, about a great actor who becomes a drunkard. At this point in his life, Barrymore was having a very rough time, doing a terrible play on the road. (*My Dear Children*, Ed). I remember taking Kate to Zanuck's office. She said: 'Of course, the one person in the world who should play this is John Barrymore.' And Zanuck said: 'I like the man very much, we've made pictures together but I don't think he is in shape to play it.' Kate was flying East to start rehearsals for a play (*The Philadelphia Story*, Ed) but she said: 'If you want me for the film, I'd love to do it, but only if Barrymore plays the lead. And, if necessary, I'll fly back to test with him.' Unfortunately, it never happened. (The play was filmed eventually in 1942 under the title *Life Begins at 8.30*, with Monty Woolley and Ida Lupino, directed by Irving Pichel. Ed.)

Rockabye (1932)

Production Company	Pathé
Director	George Cukor
Script	Jane Murfin, Kubec Glasmon. Based on the play by Lucia Bronder
Director of Photography	Charles Rosher
Editor	George Hively
Music	Max Steiner

Constance Bennett (*Judy Carrol*), Paul Lukas (*De Sola*), Joel McCrea (*Jake Pell*), Jobyna Howland (*Snooks*), Charles Middleton (*District Attorney*), Walter Pidgeon (*Commissioner Howard*), Baby June Filmer (*Lilly Bet*), Virginia Hammond (*Mrs Pell*), Walter Catlett (*Jimmie Dunn*), Clara Blandick (*Brida*).

Released in USA, November 1932. Running time, 71 min.
Distributor: RKO Pathé.

CUKOR: *Rockabye* was first completed by another director. It was a trashy story and it didn't go too well at the preview. Then I remade it in ten or twelve days, changed the leading man (Joel McCrea replaced Phillips Holmes, Ed) and put our friend Miss

Howland in it. It was still trashy but seemed all right. The first director was George Fitzmaurice, a very distinguished man. I've been taken off bigger pictures than that.

Our Betters (1933)

Production Company	RKO
Executive Producer	David O. Selznick
Director	George Cukor
Script	Jane Murfin, Harry Wagstaff Gribble. Based on the play by W. Somerset Maugham
Director of Photography	Charles Rosher
Editor	Jack Kitchin
Music	Max Steiner

Constance Bennett (*Lady Pearl Grayston*), Gilbert Roland (*Peppi D'Costa*), Charles Starrett (*Fleming Harvey*), Anita Louise (*Bessie*), Phoebe Foster (*Princess*), Grant Mitchell (*Thornton Clay*), Hugh Sinclair (*Lord Blean*), Alan Mowbray (*Lord George Grayston*), Minor Watson (*Arthur Senwick*), Violet Kemble-Cooper (*Duchess*), Tyrell Davis (*Ernest*), Virginia Howell (*Mrs Saunders*), Walter Walker (*Mr Saunders*), Harold Entwhistle (*Pole*).

Released in USA, March 1933; GB, May 1933. Running time, 72 min. Distributor: RKO Radio.

CUKOR: *Our Betters* was the wrong idea to do as a film. It had been a very amusing, hard-bitten play by Somerset Maugham and dealt with a world that they didn't know about in pictures, that of English high society. It became cheap and vulgar. Violet Kemble-Cooper was good, though, as the old lecherous Duchess, but she lacked that *vicieuse* quality that Constance Collier had brought to the role on stage.

Dinner at Eight (1933)

Production Company	M-G-M
Executive Producer	David O. Selznick
Director	George Cukor
Script	Herman J. Mankiewicz, Frances Marion. Based on the play by Edna Ferber and George S. Kaufman
Additional Dialogue	Donald Ogden Stewart
Director of Photography	William Daniels
Editor	Ben Lewis
Set Designers	Hobe Erwin, Fred Hope
Costumes	Adrian
Music	William Axt

Marie Dressler (*Carlotta Vance*), John Barrymore (*Larry Renault*), Wallace Beery (*Dan Packard*), Jean Harlow (*Kitty Packard*), Lionel Barrymore (*Oliver Jordan*), Lee Tracy (*Max Kane*), Edmund Lowe (*Dr Wayne Talbot*), Billie Burke (*Mrs Oliver Jordan*), Madge Evans (*Paula Jordan*), Jean Hersholt (*Jo Stengel*), Karen Morley (*Mrs Wayne Talbot*), Louise Closser Hale (*Hattie Loomis*), Phillips Holmes (*Ernest DeGraff*), May Robson (*Mrs Wendell*), Grant Mitchell (*Ed Loomis*), Phoebe Foster (*Miss Alden*), Elizabeth Patterson (*Miss Copeland*), Hilda Vaughn (*Tina*), Harry Beresford (*Fosdick*), Edwin Maxwell (*Mr Fitch*), John Davidson (*Mr Hatfield*), Edward Woods (*Eddie*), George Baxter (*Gustave*), Herman Bing (*Waiter*), Anna Duncan (*Dora*), Herbert Bunston, May Beatty.

Released in USA, August 1933; first shown in GB, September 1933. Running time, 110 min.
Distributor: M-G-M.

CUKOR: I shot *Dinner at Eight* in a mere twenty-four days, and it was held against me at the time. Again, it was Selznick who brought me over to Metro. It was a good play with a splendid cast. Herman Mankiewicz, a very witty scenarist, used to sympathise: 'Oh yes, it's hard work, you must be very tired. You have to get Lionel Barrymore to play a man who worries about his wife being extravagant.' (Which he was, in real life.) 'You have to make John Barrymore play a slightly broken-down actor.' (Which happened to be true.)

The dialogue was very amusing. Jean Harlow proved to be a natural comedienne. I had seen her in her early pictures, and she had been *actively* bad in them. People laughed at her in *Public Enemy*. Then I saw her in something called *Red Dust* and she was soft and feminine, with a wonderful knack of speaking funny lines as if she didn't quite understand what they meant. Marilyn had the same quality.

But when I learned that Marie Dressler was to play Carlotta Vance, I said to myself: She is not quite my idea for the part, not the way it was played on the stage by Constance Collier. Constance was enormously distinguished, she had been leading lady to Herbert Tree. But, very shrewdly, Louis B. Mayer contended that Dressler was the biggest thing in pictures, although she looked like a cook and had never played this type of part. Let me add that later in life she carried herself with great distinction. She was quite a personage in private life, even if she didn't look it. She had been a low comic on the stage, she made funny faces and made people laugh. I tried to mould her into the Ethel Barrymore type. Then I came to my senses! Suddenly I said to myself: What the hell are you trying to do? Here's a woman who's a fabulous personality. Audiences adore her. What matters is the quality. She had power, the essence of greatness, a kind of magnificence. She was more vulgar than Barrymore or Collier but you believed that she could have been a great actress. That's what one must do in pictures. Don't stand in the way. In films, it's what you *are* rather than what you *act*.

Little Women (1933)

Production Company	RKO Radio
Producer	Merian C. Cooper

Production Supervisor	Kenneth Macgowan
Director	George Cukor
Screenplay	Sarah Y. Mason and Victor Heerman. Based on the novel by Louisa May Alcott and her play *Jo's Boys*
Director of Photography	Henry Gerrard
Editor	Van Nest Polglase
Set Designer	Hobe Erwin
Costumes	Walter Plunkett
Music	Max Steiner
Sound	Frank H. Harris

Katharine Hepburn (*Jo*), Joan Bennett (*Amy*), Paul Lukas (*Professor Baer*), Frances Dee (*Meg*), Jean Parker (*Beth*), Edna May Oliver (*Aunt March*), Douglass Montgomery (*Laurie*), Henry Stephenson (*Mr Laurence*), Spring Byington (*Marmee*), Samuel S. Hinds (*Mr March*), Mabel Colcord (*Hannah*), John Lodge (*Brooke*), Nydia Westman (*Mamie*), Marion Ballou (*Mrs Kirke*), Marina de Schubert (*Flo King*), Olin Howland (*Mr Davies*), Dorothy Gray, June Filmer (*Little girls*).

Released in USA, November 1933; first shown in GB, January 1934. Running time, 115 min.
Distributor: RKO Radio.

CUKOR: This had been one of Selznick's projects before he left RKO for Metro, where he was to have his own producing unit. He had many projects like this, some of which he was not permitted to take with him. When *Little Women* came to be made, it was produced by Merian C. Cooper. Selznick, however, never lost interest in the property and sometime in the late 40s he started a remake. It didn't work out and the idea was taken over by Metro.

It turned out to be my most successful movie up to that time. It won an Oscar for the screenplay and was nominated for the best movie of the year. Its success may have led to my directing *Copperfield* and *Camille* later. I became typed as a literary director.

Sentiment was kept in place throughout. It was very honest as a picture of what America had been sixty years before. And it had superb sets and costumes. I think that after *Little Women* Selznick knew that Plunkett was the one designer for *Gone With The Wind*.

David Copperfield (1935)

Production Company	M-G-M
Producer	David O. Selznick
Director	George Cukor
Script	Howard Estabrook. Based on the novel by Charles Dickens
Adaptation	Hugh Walpole

140

Director of Photography	Oliver T. Marsh
Editor	Robert J. Kern
Art Director	Cedric Gibbons
Associate Art Directors	Merrill Pye, Edwin B. Willis
Costumes	Dolly Tree
Music	Herbert Stothart, Charles Maxwell
Special Effects	Slavko Vorkapich
Choreography	Chester Hale

W. C. Fields (*Micawber*), Lionel Barrymore (*Dan Peggoty*), Maureen O'Sullivan (*Dora*), Madge Evans (*Agnes*), Edna May Oliver (*Betsey Trotwood*), Lewis Stone (*Mr Wickfield*), Frank Lawton (*David Copperfield as a man*), Freddie Bartholomew (*David Copperfield as a boy*), Elizabeth Allan (*Mrs Copperfield*), Roland Young (*Uriah Heep*), Basil Rathbone (*Mr Murdstone*), Elsa Lanchester (*Clickett*), Jean Cadell (*Mrs Micawber*), Jessie Ralph (*Nurse Peggoty*), Lennox Pawle (*Mr Dick*), Violet Kemble-Cooper (*Jane Murdstone*), Una O'Connor (*Mrs Gummidge*), John Buckler (*Ham*), Hugh Williams (*Steerforth*), Ivan Simpson (*Limmiter*), Herbert Mundin (*Barkis*), Fay Chaldecott (*Little Em'ly as a child*), Marilyn Knowlden (*Agnes as a child*), Florine McKinney (*Little Em'ly as a woman*), Harry Beresford (*Dr Chillip*), Mabel Colcord (*Mary Ann*), Hugh Walpole (*Vicar*), Renee Gad (*Janet*).

Released in USA, January 1935; first shown in GB, March 1935. Running time, 133 min.
Distributor: M-G-M.

CUKOR: Selznick and I went to England before production work started, to gather material so the picture would look authentic. We shot some footage to be used as background, took hundreds of stills for the art department at Metro. In London, Selznick signed Sir Hugh Walpole to do the adaptation: he was a distinguished novelist and playwright as well as a Dickens expert. We also brought back several actors: Elizabeth Allan, who was adorable as David's mother; and a young actor (Peter Trent, Ed) who was to play David as a young man, but who was replaced by Frank Lawton, who was already in Hollywood.

Did you know that Charles Laughton was supposed to play Micawber? We actually shot for a few days but, although he looked marvellous, he wasn't very good in the part. He had none of the geniality and he knew it. He was finally replaced by W. C. Fields, who had a lot of Micawber in him, down to the florid speech.

All the Dickensian people were excellent. The problem was that these characters could easily become caricatures; you had to be very careful to preserve all the eccentricity, all the outward thing, yet they still had to be flesh and blood. I think we succeeded very well with Edna May Oliver and Lennox Pawle, a wonderful Mr Dick. They seemed to come out of the Phiz illustrations for the book. And Rathbone was splendid as Murdstone, no emotion whatsoever. Performances were everything in that picture. As in the novel, the second half wasn't half as good as the first. But then, the second volume is rather bad, a fatuous Victorian novel.

Sylvia Scarlett

Sylvia Scarlett (1936)

Production Company	RKO Radio
Producer	Pandro S. Berman
Director	George Cukor
Script	Gladys Unger, John Collier and Mortimer Offner. Based on the novel by Compton Mackenzie
Director of Photography	Joseph August
Editor	Jane Loring
Art Director	Van Nest Polglase
Music	Roy Webb
Sound	George D. Ellis

Katharine Hepburn (*Sylvia Scarlett*), Cary Grant (*Jimmy Monkley*), Brian Aherne (*Michael Fane*), Edmund Gwenn (*Henry Scarlett*), Dennie Moore (*Maudie*), Natalie Paley (*Lily*), Harold Cheevers (*Bobby*), Lennox Pawle (*Drunk*), Robert Adair (*Turnkey*), Lionel Pape (*Sergeant Major*), Peter Hobbes, Leonard Mudie

(*Stewards*), Harold Entwhistle (*Conductor*), Adrienne D'Ambricourt (*Stewardess*), Gaston Glass, Michael S. Visaroff (*Pursers*), Bunny Beatty (*Maid*), E. E. Clive, Edward Cooper, Olaf Hytten (*Customs Inspectors*), Dina Smirnova (*Russian*), George Nardelli (*Frenchman*).

Released in USA, January 1936; first shown in GB, May 1936. Running time, 90 min.
Distributor: RKO Radio.

CUKOR: I've been quoted as saying that a good film is a successful film. Well, there was *Sylvia Scarlett*, a flop, and still my favourite picture. Perhaps because we were all so happy while making it. We shot locations in Monterey – the locale of the story was Cornwall – and it was like a many-sided love affair. I think Cary Grant took the picture: he had a special quality that no film before had managed to capture. He was charming and crooked, very romantic. It gave him the image he needed.

Don't ask me why it was not a success. It was an unusual story but not *too* unusual. It did have unusual relationships like that of Gwenn and his mistress. Maybe because Kate was masquerading as a boy most of the time. But then, there's *As You Like It*.

Romeo and Juliet (1936)

Production Company	M-G-M
Producer	Irving Thalberg
Director	George Cukor
Script	Talbot Jennings. Based on the play by William Shakespeare
Director of Photography	William Daniels
Editor	Margaret Booth
Art Director	Cedric Gibbons
Associate Art Directors	Fredric Hope, Edwin B. Willis
Set Designers	Cedric Gibbons, Oliver Messel
Costumes	Oliver Messel, Adrian
Music	Herbert Stothart. Themes by Tchaikovsky
Choreography	Agnes DeMille
Sound	Douglas Shearer
Artistic Consultant	Oliver Messel
Literary Consultant	Professor William Strunk Jr

Norma Shearer (*Juliet*), Leslie Howard (*Romeo*), John Barrymore (*Mercutio*), Edna May Oliver (*Nurse*), Basil Rathbone (*Tybalt*), C. Aubrey Smith (*Lord Capulet*), Andy Devine (*Peter*), Ralph Forbes (*Paris*), Reginald Denny (*Benvolio*), Maurice Murphy (*Balthazar*), Conway Tearle (*Prince of Verona*), Henry Kolker (*Friar Laurence*), Robert Warwick (*Lord Montague*), Virginia Hammond (*Lady Montague*), Violet Kemble-Cooper (*Lady Capulet*), Vernon Downing (*Samson Capulet*), Ian Wolfe (*Apothecary*), Anthony Kemble-Cooper (*Gregory Capulet*),

Anthony Marsh (*Mercutio's page*), Howard Wilson (*Abraham Montague*), Carlyle Blackwell, Jr (*Tybalt's page*), John Bryan (*Friar John*), Katherine DeMille (*Rosalind*), Wallis Clark (*Town Watch*), Charles Bancroft, Jose Rubio (*Noblemen*), Dean Richmond Benton, Lita Chevret, Jeanne Hart, Dorothy Granger.

Released in USA, August 1936; first shown in GB, March 1937. Running time, 124 min.
Distributor: M-G-M.

CUKOR: *Romeo and Juliet* was Thalberg's project and it lost one million dollars for the studio. It was a prestige picture, very carefully made. Thalberg imported Messel from England to do the sets and costumes and there were all sorts of experts standing by.

The play had to be rendered clear for the general public. Our approach may not have been very original but it was serious and straightforward. The text was cut, but less than in other versions. And we had, for the most part, a good Shakespearian cast: Barrymore and Howard had both played Hamlet on stage, Rathbone had played Romeo. Only Norma Shearer was inexperienced but she was excellent in the potion scene. Maybe she and Howard were not as young as it should have been, but they acquitted themselves rather well, I think.

Barrymore was a marvellous Mercutio. But he was already having trouble remembering his lines, which made him irritable. I think it probably was his last great role. I wanted him to play the Baron in *Camille* but, by then, he was in no shape to do it. A pity, he would have been a good foil for Garbo.

Camille (1937)

Production Company	M-G-M
Producer	David Lewis
Director	George Cukor
Script	Zoë Akins, Frances Marion, James Hilton. Based on the novel and play *La Dame aux Camélias* by Alexandre Dumas *fils*
Directors of Photography	William Daniels, Karl Freund
Editor	Margaret Booth
Art Directors	Cedric Gibbons, Fredric Hope
Set Decoration	Edwin B. Willis
Costumes	Adrian
Music	Herbert Stothart
Choreography	Val Raset

Greta Garbo (*Marguerite Gauthier*), Robert Taylor (*Armand Duval*), Lionel Barrymore (*General Duval*), Henry Daniell (*Baron de Varville*), Elizabeth Allan (*Nichette*), Lenore Ulric (*Olympe*), Laura Hope Crews (*Prudence*), Jessie Ralph (*Nanine*), Rex O'Malley (*Gaston*), Russell Hardie (*Gustave*), E. E. Clive (*St Gadeau*), Douglas Walton (*Henri*), Marion Ballou (*Corinne*), Jean Brodel [Joan Leslie] (*Marie Jeanette*), June Wilkins (*Louise*), Elsie Esmond (*Madame Duval*),

Fritz Leiber, Jr (*Valentine*), Edwin Maxwell (*Doctor*), Eily Malyon (*Therese*), Mariska Aldrich (*Marguerite's friend*), May Beatty (*2nd Usher*), John Bryan (*De Musset*), Rex Evans (*Companion*), Major Harris, Bob Linden, Howard Wilson (*Armand's friends*), Eugene King (*Gypsy leader*), Adrienne Matzenauer (*Singer*), Lionel Pape (*General*), Lita Chevret (*1st girl*), Phyllis Barry (*2nd girl*), Daisy Belmore (*Shop girl*), Wilson Benge (*Attendant*), Veda Buckland (*Woman companion*), Georgia Caine (*Streetwalker*), Mabel Colcord (*Madame Barjon*), Edward Cooper (*Process server*), Robert Cory (*Coachman*), Chappel Dossett (*Priest*), Elspeth Dudgeon (*Attendant*), Effie Ellsler (*Grandma Duval*), Harold Entwhistle (*Old man*), Gerald Fielding (*Priest*), Sibyl Harris (*George Sand*), Maude Hume (*Aunt Henrietta*), Olaf Hytten (*Croupier*), Crauford Kent (*Doctor*), Charles Latorre (*Proprietor*), Mimi Lawler (*Shop girl*), Gwendolyn Logan (*Governess*), Margaret Mann (*Shop girl*), Ferdinand Munier (*Priest*), Barbara Norton (*Godmother*), Barry Norton (*Emile*), John Picorri (*Orchestra leader*), Guy Bates Post (*Auctioneer*), Frank Reicher (*Bailiff*), Harry Stubbs (*Bailiff*), Cyril Thornton (*Baron's Coachman*), Zeffie Tilbury (*Old Duchess*), Eric Wilton (*Servant*), Sue Moore, C. Montagu Show.

Released in USA, January 1937; first shown in GB, March 1937. Running time, 108 min.
Distributor: M-G-M.

CUKOR: After *Romeo and Juliet*, relations between Thalberg and Mayer were, shall we say, strained. They worked separately from each other. *Camille* was also Thalberg's picture, although his name does not appear on the credits. It seldom did. Thalberg didn't live to see the picture completed. He saw the rushes as long as he could. He said that, for the first time, Garbo appeared as flesh and blood: she danced the polka, laughed and appeared light-hearted. They made such a fuss about the fact that she laughed in *Ninotchka*. Remember the scene with Daniell at the piano? Or at the big dinner party? She always knew what she was doing, what the camera was doing, she understood, she worked hard, she was all there on the screen. What else can one say?

Holiday (1938)

Production Company	Columbia
Producer	Everett Riskin
Director	George Cukor
Script	Donald Ogden Stewart, Sidney Buchman. Based on the play by Philip Barry
Director of Photography	Franz Planer
Editors	Otto Meyer, Al Clark
Art Directors	Stephen Goosson, Lionel Banks
Costumes	Kalloch
Music	Morris Stoloff
Sound	Lodge Cunningham

Katharine Hepburn (*Linda Seaton*), Cary Grant (*Johnny Case*), Doris Nolan (*Julia Seaton*), Edward Everett Horton (*Nick Potter*), Jean Dixon (*Suzanne Potter*), Lew

Ayres (*Ned Seaton*), Henry Kolker (*Edward Seaton*), Binnie Barnes (*Laura Cram*), Henry Daniell (*Seton Cram*), Charles Trowbridge (*Banker*), George Pauncefort (*Henry*), Charles Richman (*Thayer*), Mitchell Harris (*Jennings*), Neil Fitzgerald (*Edgar*), Marion Ballou (*Grandmother*), Howard Hickman (*Man in Church*), Hilda Plowright (*Woman in Church*), Mabel Colcord (*Cook*), Raymond Lawrence, Thomas A. Brandon (*Butlers*), Bess Flowers (*Countess*), Beatrice Curtis, Beatrice Blinn (*Maids*), Harry Allen, Edward Cooper, Frank Benson, Robert Hale (*Scotsmen*), Margaret McWade (*Farmer's wife*), Frank Shannon (*Farmer*), Aileen Carlyle (*Farm girl*), Matt McHugh (*Taxi Driver*), Maurice Brierre (*Steward*), Maude Hume (*Maid*), Esther Peck (*Mrs Jennings*), Lillian West (*Mrs Thayer*), Luke Cosgrove (*Grandfather*), George Hickman (*Telegraph boy*).

Released in USA, May 1938; first shown in GB, December 1938. Running time, 93 min.
Distributor: Columbia.
GB title: *Free to Live* or *Unconventional Linda*.

CUKOR: 1928 was the year of the amateur on the Broadway stage. Philip Barry, the playwright and Arthur Hopkins, who was a wonderful director, didn't like awfully tricky acting and they invented this new style, a sort of deadpan comedy style. The big hit of the season was Barry's *Holiday* and the leading lady was Hope Williams, a very amusing-looking society girl, very distinctive; she certainly was not a very resourceful actress but she had a great deal of personality. Also in the play was Donald Ogden Stewart, a successful playwright himself. Don's wife also had a part and another society girl played his wife. The only real professional in the cast was Hope's understudy. I'm told she had very little respect for her fellow performers. Her name was Katharine Hepburn.

When Kate came to Hollywood to make films, her screen test was a scene from *Holiday*. And six years later, she found herself starring in the movie version. I never saw the play, but I remember the early talkie made from it. When the film was finished, we had an opening night party and we ran Kate's test for everybody to see what she had learned in six years!

The play was very timely in '28 when it was produced. Everybody was rich, everybody was playing the stock market and nobody had a care in the world. It seemed revolutionary then for the young hero to say: 'I don't want to make any more money, I want to enjoy my life.' It was startling, rather impertinent and very funny. As if nowadays, a young man would say 'I'm going to make a lot of money, enough of this drop-out business.' I put a lot of feeling into the movie and the dialogue was very witty. But when we made it, things weren't as funny. As a matter of fact, they were pretty grim. In a totally different climate, the picture seemed to say: The hell with rich people.

Zaza (1939)

Production Company	Paramount
Executive Producer	William Le Baron

Producer	Albert Lewin
Director	George Cukor
Assistant Director	Hal Walker
Script	Zoë Akins. Based on the play by Pierre Berton and Charles Simon
Director of Photography	Charles Lang, Jr
Editor	Edward Dymtryk
Art Directors	Hans Dreier, Robert Usher
Set Decorator	A. E. Freudeman
Costumes	Edith Head
Musical Director	Boris Morros
Musical Adviser	Phil Boutelje
Songs:	
'Zaza'	
'Hello My Darling'	Frederick Hollander, Frank Loesser and Al Hoffman
Choreography	LeRoy Prinz
Special Adviser	Alla Nazimova

Claudette Colbert (*Zaza*), Herbert Marshall (*Dufresne*), Bert Lahr (*Cascart*), Helen Westley (*Anais*), Constance Collier (*Nathalie*), Genevieve Tobin (*Florianne*), Walter Catlett (*Malardot*), Ann Todd (*Toto*), Rex O'Malley (*Bussy*), Ernest Cossart (*Marchand*), Rex Evans (*Michelin*), Robert C. Fischer (*Pierre*), Janet Waldo (*Simone*), Dorothy Tree (*Madame Dufresne*), Monty Woolley (*Fouget*), Maurice Murphy (*Henri*), Duncan Renaldo (*Animal trainer*), Olive Tell (*Jeanne Liseron*), John Sutton, Michael Brooke, Philip Warren (*Dandies*), Alexander Leftwich (*Larou*), Fredrika Brown (*Pierre's wife*), Clarence Harvey, John Power (*Conductors*), Maude Hume (*Woman*), Tom Ricketts (*Old gentleman*), Olaf Hytten (*Waiter*), Hala Linda (*Animal trainer's wife*), Frank Puglia (*Rug merchant*), Walter Soderling, Harry Allen (*Porters*), Caroline Cooke, Mayor Farrell (*Vendors*), Alice Keating (*Maid*), Dorothy Dayton, Harriette Haddon, Helaine Moler, Dorothy White, Louise Seidel (*Dancers*), Billie Bourne, Darlyn Hackley, Virginia Larsen, Grace Richey, Virginia Rooney, Lillian Ross, Peggy Russell (*Tiller girls*), Jacqueline Dax, Penny Gill, Dorothy Hamburg, Jessie Jenard, Emily La Rue, Mae Packer, Colleen Ward, Jeanne Blanche (*French girls*).

Released in USA, January 1939; first shown in GB, February 1939. Running time, 83 min.
Distributor: Paramount.

CUKOR: This old play had been a great vehicle for Mrs Leslie Carter. It was very old-fashioned by now. Paramount decided to launch their new Continental star, Isa Miranda, in the title role. But she suffered an accident and Claudette Colbert took over.

I had Zoë Akins translate directly from the French original, instead of using the standard Belasco version full of oo-la-las, chéris, amours. That's the danger when you're dealing with a French locale in Hollywood pictures: it becomes *too* picturesque! It happened to Minnelli with *Gigi* and it happened to me in *Les Girls*.

The Women (1939)

Production Company	M-G-M
Producer	Hunt Stromberg
Director	George Cukor
Script	Anita Loos, Jane Murfin. Based on the play by Clare Boothe
Directors of Photography	Oliver T. Marsh, Joseph Ruttenberg (one sequence in Technicolor)
Editor	Robert J. Kern
Art Directors	Cedric Gibbons, Wade B. Rubottom
Set Decorator	Edwin B. Willis
Music	Edward Ward, David Snell
Sound	Douglas Shearer

Norma Shearer (*Mary Haines*), Joan Crawford (*Crystal Allen*), Rosalind Russell (*Sylvie Fowler*), Mary Boland (*Countess DeLave*), Paulette Goddard (*Miriam Aarons*), Joan Fontaine (*Peggy Day*), Lucile Watson (*Mrs Moorehead*), Phyllis Povah (*Edith Potter*), Florence Nash (*Nancy Blake*), Virginia Weidler (*Little Mary*), Ruth Hussey (*Miss Watts*), Muriel Hutchison (*Jane*), Margaret Dumont (*Mrs Wagstaff*), Dennie Moore (*Olga*), Mary Cecil (*Maggie*), Marjorie Main (*Lucy*), Esther Dale (*Ingrid*), Hedda Hopper (*Dolly DuPuyster*), Mildred Shay (*Helene*), Priscilla Lawson, Estelle Etterre (*Hairdressers*), Ann Morris (*Instructress*), Mary Beth Hughes (*Miss Trimmerback*), Marjorie Wood (*Sadie, Old Maid in powder room*), Virginia Grey (*Pat*), Cora Witherspoon (*Mrs Van Adams*), Veda Buckland (*Woman*), Charlotte Treadway (*Woman's companion*), Theresa Harris (*Olive*), Virginia Howell, Barbara Jo Allen (*Receptionists*), May Beatty (*Fat woman*), May Boley (*Woman in mud mask*), Ruth Findlay (*Pedicurist*), Charlotte Wynters (*Miss Batchelor*), Aileen Pringle (*Miss Carter*), Florence Shirley (*Miss Archer*), Judith Allen (*Corset model*), Florence O'Brien (*Euphie*), Hilda Plowright (*Miss Fordyce*), Mariska Aldrich (*Singing teacher*), Jane Isebelle, Leni Lynn, Nance Lee Farrar, Jany Hope, Joey Hope (*Edith Potter's children*), Leila McIntyre (*Woman with bundles*), Dot Farley (*Large woman*), Flora Finch (*Woman window tapper*), Dorothy Sebastian, Renie Riano, Alice Keating (*Saleswomen*), Grace Goodall (*Head saleswoman*), Wilda Bennett (*Mrs Carter*), Helene Millard (*Cosmetic saleswoman*), Irene Shirley (*1st nurse*), Lilian Bond (*Mrs Erskine*), Rita Gould (*Dietician*), Effie Anderson (*2nd nurse*), Josephine Whittel (*Mrs Spencer*), Lenita Lane (*Mrs Spencer's friend*), Anne Teeman (*Make-up artist*), Aileen Carlyle (*Miss Hicks*), Nell Craig (*3rd nurse*), Bebe Anderson (*Young girl*), Shirley Chambers (*Girl in bath*), June Gittelson (*Mrs Goldstein*), Sue Moore (*1st masseuse*), Greta Meyer (*2nd masseuse*), Gladys Blake (*Miss St Claire*), Gertrude Simpson (*Stage mother*), Carole Lee Kilby (*Theatrical child*), Ruth Rickaby (*5th nurse*), Gertrude Needham (*2nd woman*), Mimi Olivera (*Manicurist*), Mabel Colcord (*Woman being massaged*), Meeka Aldrich (*4th masseuse*), Beryl Wallace, Catherine Proctor, Isobel Randolph (*Women in cabinet*), Blanche Paysson (*5th masseuse*), Winifred Harris (*Mrs North*), Lita Chevret, Dora Clemant, Ruth Alder (*Women under sunlamp*), Joan Blair (*Mrs Atkins*), Betty Blythe (*Mrs South*), Gertrude Astor (*4th nurse*), Janet McLeay (*Girl in shadowgraph*), Agnes Fraser (*1st debutante*), Mildred Coles (*2nd debutante*),

Mary Young (*Grandma*), Grace Hayle, Maude Allen (*Cyclists*), Dorothy Adams (*Miss Atkinson*), Edith Penn (*6th nurse*), Lucia LaCerte (*1st treatment girl*), Natalie Moorhead (*Woman in Modiste salon*), Marie Blake (*Stock-room girl*), Beatrice Cole (*Negligee model*), Fredericka Brown (*Head saleswoman*), Carol Hughes (*Salesgirl in Modiste salon*), Suzanne Kaaren (*Tamara*), Peggy Shannon (*Mrs Jones*), Brenda Henderson (*Mrs Jones' daughter*), Hattie Noel (*Maid on train*), Grayce Hampton (*Dowager in powder room*), Bunny Beatty (*Debutante in powder room*), Virginia Pine (*1st glamour girl*), Janet McLeay (*2nd glamour girl*), Barbara Pepper, Gladys Blake (*Tough girls*), Winifred Harris (*1st society woman*), May Beatty (*2nd society woman*), Sybil Harris (*Commentator*).

Released in USA, September 1939; first shown in GB, December 1939. Running time, 134 min.
Distributor: M-G-M.

CUKOR: My career didn't end after the *Gone With The Wind* affair. I went back to Metro, where I was not exactly Mayer's favourite director. And they were working on this play, *The Women*, by Clare Boothe. Don Stewart and Scott Fitzgerald had a hand in it, but the final result was signed by two more women, Anita Loos and Jane Murfin. It was a woman's picture – I mean there was not one man in it, not even in the street. Something like *The Merry Wives of Windsor* but very artificial and hard. I tried to remove some of the harsher things. It was done rather quickly too. It came out long before *Gone With The Wind*.

A word about the big studio system in those days. I never believed in fighting for a property. Certain novels or plays or properties were acquired for a certain star. There was the next Shearer picture or the next Crawford picture or the next Garson picture. We were in a position to choose. I wanted to work very eagerly. For instance, *The Wizard of Oz*. I don't know . . . I liked it, although I wasn't passionate about it. I started it with Mervyn LeRoy producing, then Fleming took over. But once I was involved in a project I was very passionate about the work. Nowadays, the movie industry is a whole thing of getting a property. There are no more big studios and I read with absolute fascination about these enormous productions. Who are these people? What have they done before? How did they get it together?

There were a few things that I wanted to do that didn't happen.

Susan and God (1940)

Production Company	M-G-M
Producer	Hunt Stromberg
Director	George Cukor
Script	Anita Loos. Based on the play by Rachel Crothers
Director of Photography	Robert Planck
Editor	William H. Terhune
Art Directors	Cedric Gibbons, Randall Duell, Edwin B. Willis
Music Director	Herbert Stothart

Joan Crawford (*Susan Trexel*), Fredric March (*Barry Trexel*), Ruth Hussey (*Charlotte*), John Carroll (*Clyde Rochester*), Rita Hayworth (*Leonora Stubbs*), Nigel Bruce (*Hutchins Stubbs*), Bruce Cabot (*Michael O'Hara*), Rose Hobart (*Irene Burrows*), Rita Quigley (*Blossom Trexel*), Norma Mitchell (*Paige*), Romaine Callender (*Oliver Leeds*), Marjorie Main (*Mary*), Aldrich Bowker (*Patrick*), Constance Collier (*Lady Wiggam*), Herbert Evans (*Bronson*), Coco Broadhurst (*Cowboy Joe*), Richard O. Crane (*Bob*), Don Castle (*Attendant*), Henryetta Yates (*Fifi*), Oscar O'Shea (*Sam*), Claude King (*J.F.*), Jane Dummond (*Rose*), Dan Dailey, Jr (*Homer*), Louis Payne (*Dave*), Sam Harris (*Amos*), Bobby Hale (*Tom*), Keith Hitchcock (*Scotsman*), Edward Payson (*Athlete*), Phil Tead (*Customer*), Edward Gargan (*Cab driver*), Eleanor Soohoo, Rama Bai (*Native women*), Harold Landon (*Christopher*), David Oliver (*Man at bar*), Gloria De Haven (*Enid*), Joan Brodel, Suzanne Carnahan, William Lechner, David Tillotson (*Guests*).

Released in USA, June 1940; first shown in GB, November 1940. Running time, 115 min.
Distributor: M-G-M.
GB title: *The Gay Mrs Trexel*

CUKOR: I first directed Joan Crawford when Edward Griffith took sick while making *No More Ladies*. I may have been firm with her and she didn't forget it. Then she played the heavy in *The Women* and acquitted herself rather well. She was the most photogenic girl I ever saw. She wanted me to direct her again. The play had been bought for Norma Shearer, then considered for Greer Garson; it had been played on the stage by Gertrude Lawrence. Crawford got the role. I don't think it turned out a good picture – it was still stagey.

The Philadelphia Story (1940)

Production Company	M-G-M
Producer	Joseph L. Mankiewicz
Director	George Cukor
Script	Donald Ogden Stewart; Waldo Salt (uncredited). Based on the play by Philip Barry
Director of Photography	Joseph Ruttenberg
Editor	Frank Sullivan
Art Directors	Cedric Gibbons, Wade B. Rubottom
Set Decorator	Edwin B. Willis
Music	Franz Waxman
Sound	Douglas Shearer

Katharine Hepburn (*Tracy Lord*), Cary Grant (*C. K. Dexter Haven*), James Stewart (*Macauley Connor*), Ruth Hussey (*Liz Imbrie*), John Howard (*George Kittredge*), Roland Young (*Uncle Willie*), John Halliday (*Seth Lord*), Virginia Weidler (*Dinah Lord*), Mary Nash (*Margaret Lord*), Henry Daniell (*Sidney Kidd*), Lionel Pape (*Edward*), Rex Evans (*Thomas*), Russ Clark (*John*), Hilda Plowright (*Librarian*),

150

Lita Chevret (*Manicurist*), Lee Phelps (*Bartender*), Dorothy Fay, Florine McKinney, Helene Whitney, Hillary Brooke (*Mainliners*), Claude King (*Uncle Willie's Butler*), Robert de Bruce (*Dr Parsons*), Veda Buckland (*Elsie*).

Released in USA, December 1940; first shown in GB, March 1941. Running time, 115 min.
Distributor: M-G-M.

CUKOR: This was Katharine Hepburn's comeback after she had been labelled 'box-office poison' a couple of years before. Phil Barry had written the play expressly for her; not only had she played Tracy Lord for a whole year at the Shubert Theatre in New York but she had rather a large stake in it as well. It turned out to be very successful. Everybody in the film received a nomination, including Kate and myself. But the Awards went to James Stewart and Don Stewart. Don used to say that it was the easiest job he had ever done: he had left the play intact, just opened it a little, adding one scene for James Stewart in the library, and helping to get an Oscar for Jimmy as well.

A Woman's Face (1941)

Production Company	M-G-M
Producer	Victor Saville
Director	George Cukor
Script	Donald Ogden Stewart, Elliot Paul; Christopher Isherwood (uncredited). Based on the play *Il était une fois* by Francis de Croisset and the film *En kvinnas ansikte* by Gustav Molander
Director of Photography	Robert Planck
Editor	Frank Sullivan
Art Directors	Cedric Gibbons, Wade Rubottom
Set Decorator	Edwin B. Willis
Costumes	Adrian, Gile Steele
Music	Bronislau Kaper
Choreography	Ernest Matray
Sound	Douglas Shearer

Joan Crawford (*Anna Holm*), Melvyn Douglas (*Dr Segert*), Conrad Veidt (*Torsten Barring*), Reginald Owen (*Bernard Dalvik*), Albert Bassermann (*Consul Barring*), Marjorie Main (*Emma*), Donald Meek (*Herman*), Connie Gilchrist (*Christina Dalvik*), Richard Nichols (*Lars Erik*), Osa Massen (*Vera Segert*), Charles Quigley (*Eric*), Henry Kolker (*Judge*), George Zucco (*Defence Attorney*), Henry Daniell (*Public Prosecutor*), Robert Warwick, Gilbert Emery (*Associate judges*), William Farnum (*Notary*), Sarah Padden (*Police matron*), Gwili Andre (*Gusta*), Manart Kippen (*Olaf*), Lionel Pape (*Einer*), Doris Day, Mary Ellen Popel (*Girls at Party*), Clifford Brooke (*Wickman*), Cecil Stewart (*Pianist*), Veda Buckland, Lilian Kemble-Cooper (*Nurses*), Alexander Leftwich, George Pauncefort (*Guests*), Robert

C. Fischer (*Court attendant*), Catherine Proctor (*Mrs Segerblum*), Rex Evans (*Notary*).

Released in USA, May 1941; first shown in GB, August 1941. Running time, 105 min.
Distributor: M-G-M.

CUKOR: I don't know if Isherwood worked on the scenario or not. If he did, it was before I came into the picture. This happens all the time – I don't know how many people are supposed to work on the screenplay before the final draft. It's for the Screen Writers Guild to decide who will take what credit. As far as I know, it was all Don Stewart's. He was shown a print of an Ingrid Bergman picture, made in Sweden before Selznick brought her over. It seemed like an interesting film idea: I mean, having the story told by different people in court.

I think it's an amusing picture. I've seen it recently and it holds up very well. Veidt and Bassermann were marvellous. Don wrote Basserman's dialogue with a great deal of care, as he didn't speak English too well. I think Crawford came off rather well in it. We worked very hard at it; she had a tendency to be over-emotional. I don't quite remember about the multiplication table I had her recite before the big scenes, but if she says so, it must have been so. She has a fantastic memory.

A second unit shot the final sleigh chase. Or maybe it was Victor Saville, the producer.

Two-Faced Woman (1941)

Production Company	M-G-M
Producer	Gottfried Reinhardt
Director	George Cukor
Script	Sidney H. Behrman, Salka Viertel, George Oppenheimer. Based on the play by Ludwig Fulda
Director of Photography	Joseph Ruttenberg
Special Photographic Effects	Warren Newcombe
Editor	George Boemler
Art Directors	Cedric Gibbons, Daniel B. Cathcart
Set Decorators	Edwin B. Willis, Daniel B. Cathcart
Costumes	Adrian
Music	Bronislau Kaper
Orchestrations	Leo Arnold
Choreography	Robert Alton
Sound	Douglas Shearer

Greta Garbo (*Karin/Katrin Borg*), Melvyn Douglas (*Larry Blake*), Constance Bennett (*Gliselde Vaughan*), Robert Sterling (*Dick Williams*), Roland Young (*Oscar Miller*), Ruth Gordon (*Ruth Ellis*), Frances Carson (*Miss Dunbar*), Olin Howland (*Hotel Director*), Douglas Newland, Roy Gordon (*Men*), Mary Gordon (*Wife*), Cliff

152

Danielson (*Clerk*), Hilda Plowright, Eula Guy (*Women*), Mark Daniels (*Bellboy*), Jack Arnold (*Guide*), Connie Gilchrist, Bess Flowers (*Receptionists*), Paul Leyssac (*Clerk*), Walter Anthony Merrill (*Stage manager*), George Lollier (*Cab driver*), Arno Frey (*Waiter*), Andre Cheron (*Headwaiter*), Robert Alton (*Cecil*), Lorin Raker, Tom Herbert, Grace Hayle, Emily Fitzroy (*Rhumba dancers*), Gloria De Haven, Michaele Fallon (*Debutantes*), George Calliga (*Hotel clerk*).

Released in USA, November 1941; first shown in GB, January 1942. Running time, 85 min.
Distributor: M-G-M.

CUKOR: What an uproar the picture caused! It was a rather harmless comedy, maybe a little picaresque, that was all. But the Catholic Church was outraged and Achbishop Spellman condemned it in New York. It threw Metro into a panic. Some scenes were added to make it look like the husband knows all about his wife's scheme, so that he does not commit even moral adultery.

Of course it came out at the worst possible moment and was a flop. Garbo was finished with pictures after that. Maybe if it had been some other actress ... Rosalind Russell, perhaps, or even Hepburn. Anyway, the war had closed the European market, where she had her largest following.

Her Cardboard Lover (1942)

Production Company	M-G-M
Producer	J. Walter Ruben
Director	George Cukor
Script	Jacques Deval, John Collier, Anthony Veiller, William H. Wright. Based on the play by Jacques Deval adapted by Valerie Wyngate, revised by P. G. Wodehouse
Directors of Photography	Harry Stradling, Robert Planck
Editor	Robert J. Kern
Art Directors	Cedric Gibbons, Randall Duell
Set Decorator	Edwin B. Willis
Costumes	Kalloch
Music	Franz Waxman
Song: 'I Dare You'	Burton Lane, Ralph Freed
Sound	Douglas Shearer

Norma Shearer (*Consuelo Croyden*), Robert Taylor (*Terry Trindale*), George Sanders (*Tony Barling*), Frank McHugh (*Chippie Champagne*), Elizabeth Patterson (*Eva*), Donald Meek (*Pawnbroker*), Jill Esmond (*Lizzie Hartwell*), Chill Wills (*Sam the Judge*), Roger Moore (*Simpson*), Bud Jamison (*Doorman*), Frank Elliott (*Croupier*), Olin Howland (*Frank*), Richard Crane (*Page*), Arthur Loft (*Tom*), Ottola Nesmith, Winifred Harris (*Players*), Florence Shirley (*Woman*), Alec Craig (*Danny*), Dudley Dickerson (*Porter*), Tom Herbert (*Drunk*), Johnnie Berkes (*Waiter*), Rex Evans (*Night clerk*), Gertrude Short (*Operator*), Ben Carter (*Elevator boy*), Dick Rich (*Policeman*), Fred Kelsey (*House Detective*), Raymond Hatton (*Bailiff*), Louis Mason (*Clerk*), Thurston Hall (*Mr Garthwaite*), Harry Hayden (*Attorney for hotel*), Heinie Conklin (*Drunk in courtroom*), Hobart Cavanaugh (*Detective*).

Released in USA, May 1942; first shown in GB, August 1942. Running time, 90 min.
Distributor: M-G-M.

CUKOR: This was the only time that I made a picture from one of the plays I had directed on stage. By now it was not only old-fashioned but out of place in the Pearl Harbor period. Like *Two-Faced Woman*. It proved to be Norma Shearer's last picture.

Keeper of the Flame (1943)

Production Company	M-G-M
Producer	Victor Saville
Associate Producer	Leon Gordon
Director	George Cukor
Script	Donald Ogden Stewart. Based on the novel by I. A. R. Wylie
Director of Photography	William Daniels
Special Photographic Effects	Warren Newcombe
Editor	James E. Newcom
Art Directors	Cedric Gibbons, Lyle Wheeler
Set Decorators	Edwin B. Willis, Jack Moore
Costumes	Adrian
Music	Bronislau Kaper

Spencer Tracy (*Steven O'Malley*), Katharine Hepburn (*Christine Forrest*), Richard Whorf (*Clive Spencer*), Margaret Wycherly (*Mrs Forrest*), Donald Meek (*Mr Arbuthnot*), Horace McNally [Stephen McNally] (*Freddie Ridges*), Audrey Christie (*Jane Harding*), Frank Craven (*Dr Fielding*), Forrest Tucker (*Geoffrey Midford*), Percy Kilbride (*Orion*), Howard Da Silva (*Jason Rickards*), Mary McLeod (*Janet*), Darryl Hickman (*Jeb Rickards*), Clifford Brooke (*William*), William Newell (*Piggot*), Rex Evans (*John*), Blanche Yurka (*Anna*), Craufurd Kent (*Ambassador*), Mickey Martin (*Messenger boy*), Manart Kippen, Donald Gallagher, Cliff Danielson (*Reporters*), Sam Harris, Art Howard, Harold Miller (*Men*), Jay Wrad (*Pete*), Rita Quigley (*Susan*), Dick Elliott (*Auctioneer*), Edward McWade (*Lawyer*), Irvin Lee (*Boy reporter*), Diana Dill, Gloria Tucker (*Girls*), Robert Pittard (*Tim*), Louis Mason (*Gardener*), Dr Charles Frederick Lindsley (*Minister's voice*).

Released in USA, January 1943; first shown in GB, April 1943. Running time, 100 min.
Distributor: M-G-M.

154

CUKOR: By now the war was on and everything changed. Don Stewart, who had written all these marvellous witty comedies, found this novel written by a woman, I. A. R. Wylie. As we were all good friends – Kate, Don, Spence and myself – there was no problem in getting it produced at Metro. When it was finished – I think it was already playing at the Music Hall in New York – Louis B. Mayer went to see it and came out in a fury. He may have been politically outraged by it. I don't know if Don was a Communist in those days – he was certainly very much to the Left.

It was a difficult film to grasp. I don't think we actually knew what it was all about when we were making it. It was about a very famous American about to take over the country in a Fascist plot. His wife finds out about it and fails to warn him about a certain dangerous bridge. The husband is killed but no one ever finds out that he was a traitor. It was a picture that Metro later wished they had never made.

Gaslight (1944)

Production Company	M-G-M
Producer	Arthur Hornblow, Jr
Director	George Cukor
Script	John Van Druten, Walter Reisch, John L. Balderston. Based on the play *Gas Light* by Patrick Hamilton
Director of Photography	Joseph Ruttenberg
Editor	Ralph E. Winters
Art Directors	Cedric Gibbons, William Ferrari
Set Decorators	Edwin B. Willis, Paul Huldchinsky
Special Effects	Warren Newcombe
Costumes	Irene
Music	Bronislau Kaper. Beethoven's 'Pathetique Sonata' played by Jakob Gimpel
Sound	Douglas Shearer

Charles Boyer (*Gregory Anton*), Ingrid Bergman (*Paula Alquist*), Joseph Cotten (*Brian Cameron*), Dame May Whitty (*Miss Thwaites*), Barbara Everest (*Elizabeth Tompkins*), Angela Lansbury (*Nancy Oliver*), Eustace Wyatt (*Budge*), Emil Rameau (*Maestro Guardi*), Edmund Breon (*General Huddelston*), Halliwell Hobbes (*Mr Mufflin*), Judy Ford (*Paula, aged 14*), Tom Stevenson (*Williams*), Heather Thatcher (*Lady Dalroy*), Lawrence Grossmith (*Lord Dalroy*), Charles McNaughton (*Wilkins*), Harry Adams (*Policeman*), Bobby Hale (*Lamplighter*), Phyllis Yuse (*Young girl*), Alec Craig (*Turnkey*), Leonard Carey (*Guide*), Simon Oliver (*Boy in museum*), Alix Terry (*Girl*), Ronald Bennett (*Footman*), Arthur Blake (*Butler*), Joy Harington (*Miss Pritchard*), Lillian Bronson (*Lady*), Eric Wilton (*Valet*), George Nokes (*Boy*), Guy Zanett, Al Masiello, Antonio D'Amore, Joseph Romantini, John Ardizoni (*Cabmen*), Pat Malone (*Policeman*), Frank Eldridge (*Lamplighter*), Frank Baker, Tom Hughes, Florence Benson, Wilson Benge (*Pedestrians*), Joseph North (*Policeman*), Al Ferguson, Clive Morgan, Maude Fealy, Elsie Prescott.

Released in USA, May 1944; first shown in GB, July 1944. Running time, 114 min.
Distributor: M-G-M.
GB title: *Murder in Thornton Square*

CUKOR: I returned to Metro after my discharge and my first assignment there was *Gaslight*. I think we succeeded rather well with that. It was a Victorian melodrama pure and simple, but so well done. Ingrid Bergman didn't have the frail, vulnerable quality the part of the wife required, but she was such a splendid actress she could make you believe in her.

When we were casting *Gaslight*, John Van Druten, the playwright, who was doing the screenplay, told me that Moyna McGill and her three children had arrived from England, fleeing from the blitz. Moyna was an Irish beauty who had been a leading lady of the London stage for years. It was around Christmas and Moyna and her daughter, Angela, were working in a big store in Wilshire Boulevard, making packages. I thought Angela would be good for the part of the maid. She was tested at Metro but they didn't find her sexy enough. I wanted her for the role and finally succeeded. She was a complete professional from her very first day. She was so young and pretty, and yet, in her scene with the cook, her face changed completely. Her mouth became small and sneering, she became a mean little hussy. She got a nomination for the Supporting Actress Award. She was very good in her next film, *The Picture of Dorian Gray*. But after that she was consistently miscast. I'm telling you all this because people often say that I like working exclusively with established names.

Winged Victory (1944)

Production Company	20th Century-Fox. In association with the United States Army Air Forces
Producer	Darryl F. Zanuck
Director	George Cukor
Script	Moss Hart. Based on his own play
Director of Photography	Glen MacWilliams
Editor	Barbara McLean
Production Designer	Harry Horner
Set Decorators	Lyle Wheeler, Lewis Creber
Special Effects	Fred Sersen
Costumes	Kay Nelson
Music	David Rose
Choral Director	Leonard DePaur

Lon McCallister (*Frankie Davis*), Jeanne Crain (*Helen*), Edmond O'Brien (*Irving Miller*), Jane Ball (*Jane Preston*), Mark Daniels (*Alan Ross*), Jo-Carroll Dennison (*Dorothy Ross*), Don Taylor (*Danny 'Pinky' Scariano*), Lee J. Cobb (*Doctor*), Judy Holliday (*Ruth Miller*), Peter Lind Hayes (*O'Brian*), Alan Baxter (*Major Halper*), Geraldine Wall (*Mrs Ross*), Red Buttons (*Whitey*), George Humbert (*Mr Scariano*), Barry Nelson (*Bobby Grills*), Rune Hultman (*Dave Anderson*), Richard Hogan (*Jimmy Gardner*), Phillip Bourneuf (*Col. Gibney*), Gary Merrill (*Col. Ross*), George

Reeves (*Lt. Thompson*), George Petrie (*Barker*), Alfred Ryder (*Milhauser*), Karl Malden (*Adams*), Martin Ritt (*Gleason*), Harry Lewis (*Cadet Peter Clark*), Ray Bidwell (*Officer*), Henry Rowland (*Flight Surgeon*), Carroll Riddle (*Capt. Speer*), Sascha Brastoff (*Carmen Miranda*), Archie Robbins (*Master of Ceremonies*), Jack Slate, Red Buttons, Henry Slate (*The Andrews Sisters*), Timmy Hawkins (*Irving, Jr*), Moyna MacGill (*Mrs Gardner*), Frances Gladwin (*WAC*), Sally Yarnell (*Cigarette girl*), Don Beddoe, Gil Berman, Harvey Lewis, Captain Biddle, J. Larrimore, E. Ott, Beth Willy, Mary Scott.

Released in USA, December 1944; first shown in GB, 27 January 1945. Running time, 130 min.
Distributor: 20th Century-Fox.

CUKOR: Zanuck and I were good friends then. I always found him a very interesting, mysterious man, a real picture tycoon. It was his idea that I direct *Winged Victory*. It was during the war but it wasn't really a war film – there were no scenes up in the air. It was more about training men, and the documentary parts interested me. But the story was silly; like everything that was being written at the time, it was full of patriotism and nothing else. I guess it did have a kind of charm while we were working. It was incredible to have the co-operation of the Army Air Force. All I had to say was: It would be nice to have some movement in the background during this scene. And next thing there were hundreds of men, planes landing or taking off, etc. There were a few affecting scenes with the girls. Judy Holliday was one of them. And the sets were good. Remember that Pacific island with the palm trees? It was built at Fox. But the whole thing was banal.

A Double Life (1947)

Production Company	Kanin Productions
Producer	Michael Kanin
Director	George Cukor
Assistant Director	Frank Shaw
Script	Ruth Gordon, Garson Kanin
Director of Photography	Milton Krasner
Editor	Robert Parrish
Production Designer	Harry Homer
Art Directors	Bernard Herzbrun, Harvey Gillett
Set Decorators	Russell A. Gausman, John Austin
Special Effects	David S. Horsley
Costumes	Travis Banton, Yvonne Wood
Music	Miklos Rozsa
Sound	Leslie I. Carey, Joe Lapis
Technical Adviser	
(for the *Othello* sequence)	Walter Hampden

Ronald Colman (*Anthony John*), Signe Hasso (*Brita*), Edmond O'Brien (*Bill Friend*), Shelley Winters (*Pat Kroll*), Ray Collins (*Victor Donlan*), Philip Loeb (*Max*

Lasker), Millard Mitchell (*Al Cooley*), Joe Sawyer (*Pete Bonner*), Charles La Torre (*Stellini*), Whit Bissell (*Dr Stauffer*), John Drew Colt (*Stage manager*), Peter Thompson (*Assistant stage manager*), Elizabeth Dunne (*Gladys*), Elan Edmiston (*Rex*), Art Smith, Sid Tomack (*Wig-makers*), Wilton Graff (*Dr Mervin*), Harlan Briggs (*Oscar Bernard*), Claire Carleton (*Waitress*), Betsy Blair, Janet Warren, Marjorie Woodworth (*Girls in wig shop*), Curt Conway (*Reporter*), Robert E. Keane (*2nd photographer*), Kay Lavelle (*Large woman*), Sarah Selby (*Anna*), Alexander Clark (*Barry*), Harry Bannister (*2nd actor*), Joann Dolan (*Ellen*), Joyce Matthews (*Janet*), Harry Oldridge, Nick Dennis, Barry Macollum, Frank Richards (*Stagehands*), Janet Manson, Augusta Roeland (*Girls in lobby*), Angela Clarke (*Lucy*), Paddy Chayefsky (*Photographer*), Russ Conway (*Reporter*), Fernanda Eliscu (*Landlady*), Reginald Billado (*Reporter*), Joe Bernard (*Husband*), Charles Jordan (*Bartender*), Walter McGrail (*Steve*), Joey Ray (*Boyer*), Nina Gilbert (*Woman*), Jamesson Shade, Harry Hays Morgan (*Guests*), Bruce Riley, Wayne Treadway (*Men at party*), Carl Milletaire (*Customer*), Hal Mellone (*Head usher*), William N. Bailey (*2nd detective*), Hazel Keener (*Woman*), George Sherwood (*Guest*), Ed Wragge (*3rd actor*), John Derek, Phil MacKenzie (*Police stenographers*), Elmo Lincoln (*Detective*), Buddy Roosevelt (*Fingerprint man*), Cedric Stevens (*Guest*), Don McGill (*Man at party*), Howard Mitchell (*Tailor*), Watson Downs (*Bootmaker*), Pete Sosso (*Tailor*), Albert Pollett (*Costume designer*), Countess Elektra Rozanska, Mary Worth (*Women in audience*), Ethyl May Halls (*Woman*), John Morgan, Mike Stokey, Thomas Everett Powers (*Men in audience*), John Valentine (*Man*), Laura Kasley Brooks (*Dowager*), Leander De Cordova (*Man in audience*), George Manning (*Usher*), James Linn (*Man*), Fred Hoose (*Laughing man*), George Douglas (*Man in audience*), Katharine Marlowe, Yvette Reynard, Clare Alden, Doretta Johnson, Diane Lee stewart (*Women in audience*), Michael Stark (*Man*), Maude Fealy (*Woman*), James F. Cade, Jerry Salvail (*Men in audience*). In *Othello*: Guy Bates Post, Fay Kanin, Leslie Denison, Frederic Worlock, David Bond, Arthur Gould-Porter, Virginia Patton, Boyd Irwin, Thayer Roberts, Percival Vivian. In *A Gentleman's Gentleman*: Elliott Reid, Mary Young, Georgia Caine, Percival Vivian.

Released in USA, December 1947; first shown in GB, 21 May 1948. Running time, 105 min.
Distributor: Universal.

CUKOR: This was my first picture with the Kanins. It was a most fruitful collaboration. The three of us made four pictures. I made two more with Garson, *Born Yesterday* and *It Should Happen to You*, and with Ruth I made *The Actress*, the adaptation of her play 'Years Ago'. Most of the time they wrote for people they knew very well – Hepburn, Tracy, Holliday. It's so much better this way. Now I'm not a writer, but I can contribute ideas, suggestions, dramatic effect. We worked very closely together, sometimes even through the telephone, when they were in New York, trying out scenes, lines of dialogue.

This was a melodramatic story about an actor carried away by his part. What made it interesting was the theatrical background, which was very authentic. We shot locations in New York, and I think Ronald Colman's performance should put an end to those that say there are no men in my pictures.

Edward My Son (1949)

Production Company	M-G-M
Producer	Edwin H. Knopf
Director	George Cukor
Script	Donald Ogden Stewart. Based on the play by Robert Morley and Noel Langley
Director of Photography	F. A. Young
Editor	Raymond Poulton
Art Director	Albert Junge
Special Effects	Tom Howard
Music	John Wooldridge. Played by The Philharmonia Orchestra, conducted by Sir Malcolm Sargent

Spencer Tracy (*Arnold Boult*), Deborah Kerr (*Evelyn Boult*), Ian Hunter (*Dr Larry Woodhope*), James Donald (*Bronton*), Mervyn Johns (*Harry Simpkins*), Leueen MacGrath (*Eileen Perrin*), Felix Aylmer (*Mr Hanray*), Walter Fitzgerald (*Mr Kedner*), Tilsa Page (*Betty Foxley*), Ernest Jay (*Walter Prothin*), Colin Gordon (*Ellerby*), Harriette Johns (*Phyllis Mayden*), Julian d'Albie (*Summers*), Clement McCallin (*Sgt Kenyon*).

Released in USA, May 1949; first shown in GB, 4 March 1949. Running time: 112 min.
Distributor: M-G-M.

CUKOR: It was an English play by Noel Langley which had starred Robert Morley and Peggy Ashcroft on the stage. Metro bought it for Spencer Tracy, who was miscast: the man was supposed to be ruthless and destroy everybody, even his wife, to save the son, who was a cad. It was too theatrical, the son was kept off-screen. It was the first picture I did in England.

Adam's Rib (1949)

Production Company	M-G-M
Producer	Lawrence Weingarten
Director	George Cukor
Script	Ruth Gordon, Garson Kanin
Director of Photography	George Folsey
Editor	George Boemler
Art Directors	Cedric Gibbons, William Ferrari, Henry W. Grace
Set Decorator	Edwin B. Willis
Special Effects	A. Arnold Gillespie
Music	Miklos Rozsa
Song: 'Farewell Amanda'	Cole Porter
Sound	Douglas Shearer

Spencer Tracy (*Adam Bonner*), Katharine Hepburn (*Amanda Bonner*), Judy Holliday (*Doris Attinger*), Tom Ewell (*Warren Attinger*), David Wayne (*Kip Lurie*), Jean Hagen (*Beryl Caighn*), Hope Emerson (*Olympia La Pere*), Eve March (*Grace*), Clarence Kolb (*Judge Reiser*), Emerson Treacy (*Jules Frikke*), Polly Moran (*Mrs McGrath*), Will Wright (*Judge Marcasson*), Elizabeth Flournoy (*Dr Margaret Brodeigh*), Janna da Loos (*Mary the maid*), James Nolan (*Dave*), David Clarke (*Roy*), John Maxwell (*Court clerk*), Marvin Kaplan (*Court stenographer*), Gracille LaVinder (*Police matron*), William Self (*Benjamin Klausner*), Paula Raymond (*Emerald*), De Forrest Lawrence, John Fell (*Adam's assistants*), Sid Dubin (*Amanda's assistant*), Harris Brown, Brick Sullivan (*Court attendants*), Will Stanton (*Cabbie*), Danny Harvey (*Office Boy*), Paul Cramer (*Stenographer*), Joe Bernard (*Mr Bonner*), Madge Blake (*Mrs Bonner*), Marjorie Wood (*Mrs Marcasson*), Lester Luther (*Judge Poynter*), Anna Q. Nilsson (*Mrs Poynter*), Roger David (*Hurlock*), Anthony Merrill (*Man*), Nancy Laurents (*Woman photographer*), Louis Mason (*Elderly elevator operator*), Rex Evans (*Fat man*), Charles Bastin (*Young district attorney*), Glenn Gallagher, Gil Patric, Harry Cody (*Criminal attorneys*), George Magrill, Bert Davidson (*Subway guards*), Ray Walker (*Photographer*), Tom Noonan (*Reporter*), Michael Kostrick, Tom Quinn, Dwight Martin, Ralph Montgomery (*Photographers*), Wilson Wood, David McMahon, Dan Quigg, Dick Cogan (*Reporters*).

Released in USA, November 1949; first shown in GB, February 1950. Running time: 101 min.
Distributor: M-G-M.

CUKOR: Sometimes, when I see some of my earlier pictures, I wince. But not *Adam's Rib*, I think it's still lovely. We tried extremely long takes in the picture. There's a scene between Kate and Judy Holliday that runs for more than seven minutes without a cut. I thought it was better to build the intensity of the scene. Also, the scene when David Wayne tries to seduce Kate is done in one very long take.

Holliday was fresh from her Broadway success in *Born Yesterday*. She objected to only one line in the dialogue, when she tells how her husband told her: Shut up, Fatso. She was right to worry. Harry Cohn, who had bought the picture rights to the play, didn't want her to repeat her role in the movie, he thought she was too fat. The line stayed but Judy was carefully photographed and wore flattering dresses in the last scenes, so all one could remember afterwards was how funny her performance was.

A Life of Her Own (1950)

Production Company	M-G-M
Producer	Valdemar Vetluguin
Director	George Cukor
Script	Isobel Lennart
Director of Photography	George Folsey
Editor	George White

Montage Sequence	Peter Ballbusch
Art Directors	Cedric Gibbons, Arthur Lonergan
Set Decorators	Edwin B. Willis, Henry W. Grace
Music	Bronislau Kaper
Musical Director	Johnny Green
Sound	Douglas Shearer

Lana Turner (*Lily Brannel James*), Ray Milland (*Steve Harleigh*), Tom Ewell (*Tom Caraway*), Louis Calhern (*Jim Leversoe*), Ann Dvorak (*Mary Ashlon*), Barry Sullivan (*Lee Gorrance*), Margaret Phillips (*Nora Harleigh*), Jean Hagen (*Maggie Collins*), Phyllis Kirk (*Jerry*), Sara Haden (*Smitty*), Hermes Pan (*Lily's dance partner*), Carol Brannan (*First model*), Tom Seidel (*Bob Collins*), Bethe Douglas, Roberta Johnson, Alice Wallace, Bunny Waters, Pat Davies, Dorothy Abbott, Bridget Carr, Charlene Hardey, Marlene Hoyt (*Stock models*), Hilda Plowright (*Desk clerk*), Louis Mason (*Porter*), Florence Cunningham (*Spinster*), Elizabeth Flournoy (*Caraway receptionist*), Georgia Pelham (*1st model*), Elaine Edwards (*Girl coming out*), Helen Eby-Rock, Marjorie Liszt and Donie Bussey (*Telephone clerks*), Betty Jane Howarth, Sue Carlton (*Girls waiting*), John Crawford (*Photographer*), Dorothy Tree (*Caraway secretary*), Ann Robin, Pat Hall (*Girls showing legs*), Geraldine Wall (*Hosiery woman*), Robert Emmet Keane, Richard Anderson (*Hosiery men*), Sally Cooper (*Kathy Ralston*), Chris Olson (*Maggie's son*), Wilson Wood (*Cab driver*), John Butler (*Cigar clerk*), Lurene Tuttle (Vogue *secretary*), Maura Murphy (Vogue *receptionist*), Ann Hunter (*Miss Lamson*), Madge Blake (*Matron*), Marjorie Wood (*Desk clerk*), Gilbert Herman (*Artist*), Joe Bautista (*Houseboy*), David Hydes (*Hotel waiter*), Percy Helton (*Hamburger proprietor*), Tommy Bernard (*Son*), Myron Welton (*Other boy*), Sarah Padden (*Overseer*), Betty Seland (*Voice*), Kathleen Freeman (*Peg*), Gertrude Graner (*Woman photographer*), Carol West (*Girl on street*), Clifford Brooke (*Waiter*), Whit Bissell (*Rental agent*), Harry Barris (*Piano player*), Harry Ellerbe (*1st man*), Frank Gerstle (*2nd man*), Ray Walker, Keith McConnell (*Men at piano*), Michael Dugan (*Man at party*), Ken Duncan (*Man*), Beverly Campbell (*Girl at party*), James Cross (*Drunk*), Rothelma Stevens (*Kay*), Claude Stroud (*Man with champagne*), Marlo Dwyer (*Gravel-voiced dame*), James Horne, William Cabanne (*Male models*), John Albright (*Coffee delivery boy*), Mickey Martin (*United Parcel boy*), Johnny Walsh (*Western Union boy*), Major Sam Harris (*Man model*), John Maxwell (*Executive*), David Bond (*Photographer*), Glen Gregory (*Ventriloquist*), Frankie Darro (*Bellboy*), Andre Charisse, Robert Cauterio, George Dee, Daniel De Johghe (*Men in* Vogue *office*), Dianthe Pattison, Janet Fay, Claudette Thornton (*Girls playing canasta*), Bert Keyes (*Miner*), Barbara Darrow, Alice Darrow (*Girls on mezzanine*), Queenie Leonard (*Hotel matron*), Margaret Bert (*Hotel maid*), Victor Cutler (*Young man*), Joan Valerie, Kerry O'Day, Carol Brewster, Beverly Thompson, Lee Lynn, Meredith Leeds, Sue Casey (*Girls at party*), Kenny Garcia, Arthur Loew, Jr, Peter Thompson, Walter McGrail (*Men at party*), Paul Kramer (*Airport gateman*).

Released in USA, August 1950; first shown in GB, October 1950. Running time, 150 min., cut first to 110 min. and finally to 108 min.
Distributor: M-G-M.

162

CUKOR: Cut to ribbons but an awful movie in any case. Even the ending was changed: Turner was supposed to commit suicide. I've tried to forget it.

Born Yesterday (1950)

Production Company	Columbia
Producer	S. Sylvan Simon
Director	George Cukor
Assistant Director	Earl Bellamy
Script	Albert Mannheimer. Based on the play by Garson Kanin
Dialogue Supervisor	David Pardoll
Director of Photography	Joseph Walker
Editor	Charles Nelson
Art Directors	William Kiernan, Harry Horner
Music	Frederick Hollander
Musical Director	Morris Stoloff
Sound	Jack Goodrich

Judy Holliday (*Billie Dawn*), Broderick Crawford (*Harry Brock*), William Holden (*Paul Verrall*), Howard St John (*Jim Devery*), Frank Otto (*Eddie*), Larry Oliver (*Norval Hedges*), Barbara Brown (*Mrs Hedges*), Grandon Rhodes (*Sanborn*), Claire Carleton (*Heln*), Smoki Whitfield (*Bootblack*), Helyn Eby Rock (*Manicurist*), William Mays (*Bellboy*), David Pardoll (*Barber*), Mike Mahoney (*Elevator operator*), Paul Marion (*Interpreter*), John L. Morley, Ram Singh and Bhogwan Singh (*Natives*), Charles Cane (*Policeman*).

Released in USA, November 1950; first shown in GB, April 1951. Running time: 102 min.
Distributor: Columbia.

CUKOR: The script was really written by Garson Kanin himself, although it was signed by someone else. The play was opened up with some locations in Washington, D.C. It was a picture that we rehearsed carefully, as if we were going on stage with it. The reason for this was that Judy Holliday had played Billie Dawn for years and knew that play backwards, while Holden and Crawford were new to it. All three roles had to be letter-perfect as that's *all* there is to the play. I wanted ensemble acting.

The Model and the Marriage Broker (1951)

Production Company	20th Century-Fox
Producer	Charles Brackett
Director	George Cukor
Script	Charles Brackett, Walter Reisch, Richard Breen

Dialogue	James Vincent
Director of Photography	Milton Krasner
Editor	Robert Simpson
Art Directors	Lyle Wheeler, John De Cuir
Set Decorators	Thomas Little, Walter M. Scott
Special Effects	Fred Sersen
Music	Cyril Mockridge
Musical Director	Lionel Newman
Sound	Eugene Grossman, Roger Heman

Jeanne Crain (*Kitty*), Scott Brady (*Matt*), Thelma Ritter (*Mae Swazey*), Zero Mostel (*Wixted*), Michael O'Shea (*Doberman*), Helen Ford (*Emmy*), Frank Fontaine (*Johannson*), Dennie Moore (*Mrs Gingras*), John Alexander (*Mr Perry*), J. C. Flippen (*Chancellor*), Bunny Bishop (*Alice*), Kathryn Card (*Mrs Kuschner*), Maude Prickett (*Delia Seton*), Athalie Daniell (*Trudy*), Dennis Ross (*Joe*), Ken Christy (*Mr Kuschner*), Shirley Mills (*Ina Kuschner*), Eve March (*Miss Eddy*), Tommy Noonan (*Young clerk*), Jacqueline French (*Miss Perry*), Edna May Wonacott (*Miss Perry*), June Hedin (*Miss Perry*), Robert Board (*Usher*), Tom Martin (*Fountain attendant*), Blyth Daly (*Receptionist*), Elizabeth Flournoy (*Saleswoman*), Nancy Kulp (*Hazel*), Zori Jennings, Lucille Barner, Joan Roberts, Diana Mumby (*Models*), Harris Brown, Frank Ferguson (*Conventioneers*), John Reed (*Western Union boy*), Harry Carter (*Big Doug*), Joyce MacKenzie (*Doris*), Mae Marsh (*Woman*).

Released in USA, November 1951; first shown in GB, February 1952. Running time: 103 min.
Distributor: 20th Century-Fox.

The Marrying Kind (1952)

Production Company	Columbia
Producer	Bert Granet
Director	George Cukor
Assistant Director	Earl Bellamy
Second Unit Director	Harry Horner
Script	Ruth Gordon, Garson Kanin
Director of Photography	Joseph Walker
Editor	Ralph Nelson
Art Director	John Meehan
Set Decorator	William Kiernan
Music	Hugo Friedhofer
Musical Director	Morris Stoloff
Sound	Jack Goodrich

Judy Holliday (*Florence Keefer*), Aldo Ray (*Chet Keefer*), Madge Kennedy (*Judge Anna Carroll*), Sheila Bond (*Joan Shipley*), John Alexander (*Howard Shipley*), Rex Williams (*George Bastian*), Phyllis Povah (*Mrs Derringer*), Peggy Cass (*Emily*

Bundy), Mickey Shaughnessy (*Pat Bundy*), Griff Barnett (*Charley*), Susan Halloran (*Ellen*), Christie Olsen (*Joey No. 1*), Barry Curtis (*Joey No. 2*), Wallace Acton (*Newhouse*), Elsie Holmes (*Marian*), Joan Shawlee (*Girl dancing partner*), Thomas B. Henry (*Mr Jenner*), Frank Ferguson (*Mr Quinn*), Don Mahin (*Roy*), Larry Blake (*Benny*), Tom Farrell (*Cliff*), Gordon Jones (*Steve*), John Elliott (*Minister*), Joe McGuinn (*Bus driver*), Richard Gordon (*Lawyer*), Patrick Butler (*Kid*), Malna Mills (*Charlotte*), Nancy Kulp (*Edie*), Peggy Walker (*Gloria*), Mary Chamberlain (*Leona*), Jean Wardley (*Peggy*), James MacColl (*Man in subway*), Charles Buchinski [Charles Bronson] (*Eddie*), George Auld (*Spec*), Raymond Largay (*Postmaster General*), Frank Kreig (*Hank*), Robert G. Hartley, Charles S. Brewer, Johnny Kiado (*Musicians*), Carl Laviness, Alan Marston, Alexis Davidoff, Jeffrey Sayre, John Sheffield, Margaret Roberts, Shirlee Allard, Vera Burnett, Terry Kingston, Charles Morton, Ethan Laidlaw, Guy Teague, Allen Pinson.

Released in USA, March 1952; first shown in GB, November 1952. Running time: 93 min.
Distributor: Columbia.

CUKOR: Maybe the picture suffered from being too serious, the child's death was tragic. It was a bold idea to mix tragedy and comedy, but that's the way it happens in real life, doesn't it? Columbia had its doubts, they tried to tilt in favour of comedy, not realizing that the Kanins had a perfectly balanced script to start with.

The role of the husband was to go to Sid Caesar, originally. But I saw a test of Aldo Ray and, although it wasn't very good, he did have a very individual quality. Like Holliday, he was overweight, but his eyes and his voice were very special. There was a silent scene in the test when he sat on the floor and threw cards around that made me believe he could play it. He was signed, after the Kanins agreed, and he started to lose weight.

At first, he was terrified, just like Shelley Winters had been in *A Double Life*. It took a few days for him to regain his self-confidence. You see, he was new to acting, had done a football picture before at Columbia, that's all (*Saturday's Hero*, Ed). Then he did a scene with Judy in which he didn't say a word, just looked at her and did small gestures. He was getting into the role, slowly. He was excellent in the comedy scenes and finally the tragic scenes went without a hitch. Remember when he breaks down and cries?

I made one other picture with him, *Pat and Mike*, a comedy about golf. He played a punch-drunk fighter. He was very funny. He should have become a star.

Pat and Mike (1952)

Production Company	M-G-M
Producer	Lawrence Weingarten
Director	George Cukor
Script	Ruth Gordon, Garson Kanin
Director of Photography	William Daniels
Editor	George Boemler

Montage Sequences	Peter Ballbusch
Art Directors	Cedric Gibbons, Urie McCleary
Set Decorators	Edwin B. Willis, Hugh Hunt
Special Effects	Warren Newcombe
Music	David Raksin
Sound	Douglas Shearer

Spencer Tracy (*Mike Conovan*), Katharine Hepburn (*Pat Pemberton*), Aldo Ray (*Davie Hucko*), William Ching (*Collier Weld*), Sammy White (*Barney Grau*), George Mathews (*Spec Cauley*), Loring Smith (*Mr Beminger*), Phyllis Povah (*Mrs Beminger*), Gussie Moran, Babe Didrikson Zaharias, Don Budge, Alice Marble, Frank Parker, Betty Hicks, Beverly Hanson, Helen Dettweiler (*Themselves*), Charles Buchinski [Charles Bronson] (*Hank Tasling*), Frank Richards (*Sam Garsell*), Jim Backus (*Charles Barry*), Chuck Connors (*Police Captain*), Joseph E. Bernard (*Gibby*), Owen McGiveney (*Harry MacWade*), Lou Lubin (*Waiter*), Carl Switzer (*Bus Boy*), William Self (*Pat Pemberton's Caddy*), Jeanne Wardsley (*Secretary*), Lois Messler (*Assistant Coach*), Billy McLean, Frankie Darro, Paul Brinegar, 'Tiny' Jimmie Kelly (*Caddies*), Mae Clark, Helen Eby-Rock, Elizabeth Holmes (*Women golfers*), Gil Patric (*Caddy*), Hank Weaver (*Commentator*), Tony Hughes (*Press official*), Kay English, Jerry Schumacher, Sam Pierce, Bill Lewin, A. Cameron Grant (*Reporters*), King Mojave (*Linesman*), Val Ray (*Tennis umpire*), Tom Ferrandini (*Tennis linesman*), Louis Mason (*R. R. Conductor*), Tom Harmon (*Sportscaster*).

Released in USA, June 1952; first shown in GB, 4 October 1952. Running time: 95 min.
Distributor: M-G-M.

The Actress (1953)

Production Company	M-G-M
Producer	Lawrence Weingarten
Director	George Cukor
Assistant Director	Jack Greenwood
Script	Ruth Gordon. Based on her play *Years Ago*
Director of Photography	Harold Rosson
Editor	George Boemler
Art Directors	Cedric Gibbons, Arthur Lonergan
Set Decorators	Edwin B. Willis, Emile Kuri
Special Effects	Warren Newcombe
Music	Bronislau Kaper
Costumes	Walter Plunkett
Sound	Douglas Shearer

Spencer Tracy (*Clinton Jones*), Jean Simmons (*Ruth Gordon Jones*), Teresa Wright (*Annie Jones*), Anthony Perkins (*Fred Whitmarsh*), Ian Wolfe (*Mr Bagley*), Kay

Williams (*Hazel Dawn*), Mary Wickes (*Emma Glavey*), Norma Jean Nilsson (*Anna*), Dawn Bender (*Katherine*), Keith Hitchcock (*Comedian*), Erville Anderson (*Mike McGrath*), Erwin Volze (*Mr Donough*), Jackie Coogan (*Man Heckler*), Ellen Morgan (*Woman*), Matt Moore (*Waiter*), Mitchell Lewis (*Stage Doorman*), Walter Reed (*John Craig*), Lou Mason (*Mr Sparrow*).

Released in USA, June 1953; first shown in GB, November 1953. Running time: 90 min.
Distributor: M-G-M.

CUKOR: This was a biographical play by Ruth Gordon. The picture was somewhat modified by the producer, the girl was made less tough, more lovable. But the whole point is that young people can be ruthless. Like Ruth herself was, otherwise she would have never left home.

It's a quiet, intimate picture of family life around 1917. We did the art direction from actual photographs. Most of the action takes place in the kitchen and it was a realistic small kitchen. Changed a little but certainly not romanticized.

It Should Happen to You (1954)

Production Company	Columbia
Producer	Fred Kohlmar
Director	George Cukor
Assistant Director	Earl Bellamy
Script	Garson Kanin
Director of Photography	Charles Lang
Editor	Charles Nelson
Art Director	John Meehan
Set Decorator	William Kiernan
Music	Frederick Hollander
Musical Director	Morris Stoloff
Orchestrations	Arthur Morton
Sound	Lodge Cunningham

Judy Holliday (*Gladys Glover*), Peter Lawford (*Evan Adams III*), Jack Lemmon (*Pete Sheppard*), Michael O'Shea (*Brod Clinton*), Vaughan Taylor (*Entrikin*), Connie Gilchrist (*Mrs Riker*), Walter Klavun (*Bert Piazza*), Whit Bissell (*Robert Grau*), Arthur Gilmore (*Don Toddman*), Rex Evans (*Con Cooley*), Haywood Hale Brown (*Sour man*), Ralph Dumke (*Beckhard*), Lenny Bremen (*Allie*), Chick Chandler (*Engineer*), Frank Nelson (*Salesman*), Mary Young (*Old lady*), Cora Witherspoon (*Saleslady*), Kit Guard (*Man*), James Nusser, Edwin Chandler, Stan Malotte, Robert Berger, Earl Keen, George Becwar, Tom Hennesy, Leo Curley (*Board Members*), Ted Thorpe, Tom Cound (*Assistant photographers*), Sandra Lee, Stephany Hampson (*Teenagers*), Harold J. Kennedy (*Photographer*), James Hyland (*Bartender*), Margaret McWade (*Elderly lady*), Louis Mason (*1st person*), Marjorie Woodworth (*Woman*), Almeda Fowler (*3rd person*), Pat Waltz (*3rd photographer*),

It Should Happen to You

Roger Pace (*Photographer*), George Kitchel (*Lieutenant*), Don Richards (*Photographer*), Jack Krushen (*Joe*), Stanley Orr (*Make-up man*), Herbert Lytton (*Sound man*), Howard Price, Patrick Miller, Mort Mills (*Photographers*), Chris Alcaide, John Veitch, Grant Scott (*Air force enlisted men*), John Saxon (*Young man in park*), Melville Cooper (*Dr Manning*), Ilka Chase, Constance Bennett, Wendy Barrie (*Themselves*).

Released in USA, March 1954; first shown in GB, February 1954. Running time: 87 min.
Distributor: Columbia.

CUKOR: I have to work from the script. It tells me what the style of each scene should be, if it must be done lightly or seriously. It's my theatre background. And yet there is always room for improvisation. For instance, Jack Lemmon in *It Should Happen to You*. While rehearsing a fight scene with Judy Holliday, he began to double up with pain. I always get a belly ache when I'm upset, he said. We put it in the scene, it made it more true. I think it's still in the final print.

You should incorporate traits of the actor into the part. When Jean Simmons was playing in *The Actress* there was a tense scene with Tracy playing her father, when she couldn't help giggling from sheer nervousness. She always did. We put it in.

A Star is Born (1954)

Production Company	Transcona Enterprises
Producer	Sidney Luft
Associate Producer	Vern Alves
Director	George Cukor
Assistant Directors	Earl Bellamy, Edward Graham, Russell Llewellyn
Script	Moss Hart. Based on the screenplay by Dorothy Parker, Alan Campbell and Robert Carson for the film *A Star is Born* (1937). Original story: William A. Wellman and Robert Carson. Inspired by the film *What Price Hollywood?*, scenario by Adela Rogers St John
Director of Photography	Sam Leavitt (CinemaScope)
Colour Process	Technicolor
Technicolor Colour Consultant	Mitchell G. Kovaleski
Special Colour Consultant	Hoyningen-Huene
Editor	Folmar Blangsted
Production Designer	Gene Allen
Art Director	Malcolm Bert
Set Decorator	George James Hopkins
Special Effects	H. F. Koenekamp
Music	Harold Arlen
Musical Director	Ray Heindorf
Songs:	
'Gotta Have Me Go With You'	
'The Man That Got Away'	
'Here's What I'm Here For'	
'It's a New World'	
'Someone at Last'	
'Lose That Long Face'	Sung by Judy Garland. Music: Harold Arlen. Lyrics: Ira Gershwin
'Born in a Trunk'	Sung by Judy Garland. Music and lyrics: Leonard Gershe. Art Direction and Costumes: Irene Sharaff. Directed by Richard Barstow and Roger Edens
Vocal Arrangements	Jack Cathcart
Costumes	Jean Louis, Mary Ann Nyberg
Choreography	Richard Barstow
Sound	Charles B. Lang, David Forrest

169

Judy Garland (*Esther Blodgett later Vicki Lester*), James Mason (*Ernest Sidney Gubbins* alias *Norman Maine*), Jack Carson (*Matt Libby*), Charles Bickford (*Oliver Niles*), Tommy Noonan (*Danny McGuire*), Lucy Marlow (*Lola Lavery*), Jerry DeCoe, Wayne Taylor, Melvin Pogue, Janet Stewart, Sylvia Arslan, Colette McMahon (*Autograph seekers*), George Fisher (*Announcer*), Jim Hyland (*Assistant Announcer*), Joan Shawlee (*Woman Announcer*), Sam Colt (*Stage manager*), Jay Johnson (*Musician*), James Brown (*Williams*), Tom Kingston, George Kitchell, Robert Dumas, Duff Whitney (*Reporters*), Irving Bacon (*Manservant*), Louis Mason (*Doorman*), Frank Puglia (*Head Waiter*), Michael Hathaway (*Agent*), Havis Davenport (*Starlet*), Elmera Smith (*Pasadena girl*), Jack Pepper (*Chef*), Dub Taylor (*Driver*), Louis Jean Heidt (*Director*), Don Richards (*Cameraman*), Bob Jellison (*Eddie*), Al Ebens (*Proprietor*), Marjorie Woodworth (*Woman*), Don Shelton (*TV Director*), Robert Stevenson (*Boom man*), Chick Chandler (*Man in car*), Kathryn Card (*Landlady*), Geraldine Wall (*Woman*), Nancy Kulp, Mary Young (*Rooming house women*), Alan DeWitt, Rudy Anders, Joe Dougherty (*Make-up men*), Ross Carmichael (*Photographer*), Lotis Robb (*Miss Markham*), Blythe Daly (*Miss Fusselow*), Leonard Penn (*Director*), Eddie Dew (*Cameraman*), Charles Conrad, George Becwar (*Assistant Directors*), Charles Halton (*1st Cashier*), Joseph Mell (*2nd Cashier*), Olin Howlin (*Charlie*), Harry Seymour, Grandon Rhodes, Don Dillaway, Don Beddoe (*Men at preview*), Red Thorpe, David Armstrong, Bob Hoy, Larry Rio (*Sound men*), Al Thompson, Oscar Blank (*Vagrants*), Emerson Treacy (*Justice of Peace*), Willis Bouchey (*Director McBride*), John Carlyle (*Assistant Director*), Robert Haines (*Second Assistant*), Mike Kostrick (*Cameraman*), Ruth Bradee, Shirley Whitney, Jean Engstrom, Almeda Fowler, Mae Marsh, Arlene Karr, Paul Levitt, Rodney Bell, Richard Bauman, Marshall Bradford (*Malibu party guests*), Eric Wilton (*Butler*), Hazel Shermet (*Libby's secretary*), John Monaghan (*Male secretary*), Louis Tomei, Carey Loftin (*Signboard men*), Strother Martin (*Express man*), Grady Sutton (*Carver*), Rex Evans (*M.C.*), Susan Ettinger (*Amanda Blake*), Richard Webb (*Wallace*), Steve Wyman (*Nigel Peters*), Tom Cound (*Price Waterhouse man*), Mort Mills (*Make-up man*), Kay Ridhl (*Hairdresser*), Tristram Coffin (*Director*), Henry Kulky (*Cuddles*), Riza Royce (*Secretary*), Tom Blakiston (*Young man*), Pat O'Malley, Gertrude Astor (*People at race track*), Valerie Vernon (*Marian*), Pat Sexton (*Bert*), Jack Ellis (*Pinkerton Detective*), Frank Ferguson (*Judge*), Timothy Farrell (*Bailiff*), Percy Helton (*Rodriguez*), Benny Burt, Ralph Volkie, Robert Strong (*Courtroom reporters*), Josephine Whittell, Sheila Bromley, Elizabeth Flournoy, Ruth Warren, Cele Kirk, Eileene Stevens, Helen Eby-Rock, Hilda Plowright, Ezelle Poule (*Women at funeral*), Harte Wayne, Louis Mason, Frank Kreig, Paul Brinegar (*Men at funeral*), Dale Van Sickel, Don Richards, Robert Dumas, Jean Woodley (*Reporters at Shrine Auditorium*), Pat Miller, Al Hill, Frank Marlowe, Charles Morton, Gordon Finn (*Photographers at Shrine Auditorium*), Wilton Graff (*M.C.*), Walter Rode (*Cop in courtroom*). 'Born in a Trunk' Number: Dick Simmons (*Producer*), Joe Greene (*1st agent*), Joe Hamilton (*2nd agent*), Phil Arnold (*3rd agent*), Jack Baker (*Father*), Ila McAvoy (*Mother*), Nadene Ashdown (*Esther at 6*), Heidi Meadows (*Esther at 3*), Jack Kenney (*1st nightclub man*), Dick Ryan (*2nd nightclub man*).

Released in USA, October 1954; first shown in GB, 29 May 1955. Running time: 182 min., then 154 min., finally 135 min.
Distributor: Warner Bros.

170

CUKOR: The picture was mangled after the première. They thought it was over-long, which it probably was, except that everything was in the right place. So they cut important scenes to make room for the endless 'Born in a Trunk' number, which I did not direct – it was put together by the art director and the choreographer – and they removed 'Lose That Long Face' which was essential to the scene with Bickford in her dressing-room.

It was my first picture in CinemaScope and colour. There were all these theories about what you could and could not do with the wide screen. You weren't supposed to cut too fast with CinemaScope, audiences would get dizzy. Well, I did, right at the very beginning. As for colour, I was assisted by a marvellous artist, the late George Hoyningen-Huene, one of the great photographers of the century, a man of impeccable taste who worked for *Vogue* and *Harper's Bazaar* for many years. He, Gene Allen – who became my art director – and myself worked together from then on. Except for pictures that I inherited like *Justine* or *Song Without End*. Cecil Beaton came with *My Fair Lady*. In all our pictures together we tried different experiments. A director can benefit enormously from this type of collaboration. I don't like splashy lights all over the set, I want colour to be logical.

There was no prototype for Garland except Garland herself. You just asked me if Mrs 'Pat' Campbell was the inspiration for all those bitchy heroines. Well, you don't take somebody full grown, you collect through several years of experience and you assemble all these, you put together a performance. Laurette Taylor's daughter, Marguerite, came to see Garland work in *A Star is Born*. She wrote this brilliant biography of her mother, the best theatrical memoir I have ever read. And she said: 'You know, if my book is ever done as a play or a movie, the one to play Laurette is Garland.' When I told Garland what she had said, I discovered that she had never seen Laurette perform. She wasn't conscious of it, maybe I wasn't either, but I had seen Laurette work and some of the things that I saw her do, some of her desperation, her vulnerability, had passed through me to Garland. I find that certain things that impress you somehow show up in your work on the screen. It all becomes a pastiche of your past experience.

Bhowani Junction (1956)

Production Company	M-G-M
Producer	Pandro S. Berman
Director	George Cukor
Assistant Director	James Ware
Script	Sonya Levien, Ivan Moffat. Based on the novel by John Masters
Director of Photography	F. A. Young (CinemaScope)
Colour Process	Eastman Colour
Colour Consultant	Hoyningen-Huene
Editors	Frank Clarke, George Boemler
Art Directors	Gene Allen, John Howell
Special Effects	Tom Howard
Costumes	Elizabeth Haffenden

| Music | Miklos Rozsa |
| Sound | Alexander Fisher |

Ava Gardner (*Victoria Jones*), Stewart Granger (*Colonel Rodney Savage*), Bill Travers (*Patrick Taylor*), Abraham Sofaer (*Surabhai*), Francis Matthews (*Ranjit Kasel*), Marne Maitland (*Govindaswami*), Peter Illing (*Ghanshyam*), Edward Chapman (*Thomas Jones*), Freda Jackson (*The Sadani*), Lionel Jeffries (*Lt Graham McDaniel*), Alan Tilvern (*Ted Dunphy*), Raymond Francis (*Capt Cumberly*), Dharma Rajah Emmanuel (*Sentry*), Eric Corrie (*Man-at-arms*), Harold Kasket (*Proprietor of restaurant*).

Released in USA, May 1956; first shown in GB, August 1956. Running time, 110 min.
Distributor: M-G-M.

CUKOR: There were several scenes that were cut by the censor. I had a sort of 'Lubitsch touch' in one scene: Ava Gardner brushing her teeth with Granger's toothbrush. It was cut. Also, a very passionate scene in bed with Bill Travers, where we kept her face in close-up, something like *Les Amants*. It was a big film, thousands of extras. I think of DeMille now as a great story-teller. I don't really know if I'm very good with story; I'd rather have characters.

Les Girls (1957

Production Company	M-G-M
Producer	Sol C. Siegel
Associate Producer	Saul Chaplin
Director	George Cukor
Assistant Director	Robert Saunders
Script	John Patrick. Based on a story by Vera Caspary
Director of Photography	Robert Surtees (CinemaScope)
Colour Process	Metrocolor
Colour Consultant	George Hoyningen-Huene
Editor	Ferris Webster
Art Directors	William A. Horning, Gene Allen
Set Decorators	Edwin B. Willis, Richard Pefferle
Special Effects	Lee Le Blanc
Musical Director	Adolph Deutsch
Orchestrations	Alexander Courage, Skip Martin
Vocal Supervisor	Robert Tucker
Songs:	Cole Porter
'Les Girls'	Sung by Gene Kelly, Kay Kendall, Mitzi Gaynor, Taina Elg
'Ladies in Waiting'	Sung by Kay Kendall, Mitzi Gaynor, Taina Elg
'Ça c'est l'Amour'	Sung by Mitzi Gaynor, Taina Elg
'You're Just Too Too'	Sung by Gene Kelly, Kay Kendall

'Why Am I So Gone About That Girl?'	Sung by Gene Kelly
Costumes	Orry-Kelly
Choreography	Jack Cole
Sound	Wesley C. Miller

Gene Kelly (*Barry Nichols*), Kay Kendall (*Lady Sybil Wren*), Mitzi Gaynor (*Joy Henderson*), Taina Elg (*Angele Ducros*), Jacques Bergerac (*Pierre Ducros*), Leslie Phillips (*Sir Gerald Wren*), Henry Daniell (*Judge*), Patrick MacNee (*Sir Percy*), Stephen Vercoe (*Mr Outward*), Philip Tonge (*Associate Judge*), Maurice Marsac (*French theatre manager*), Owen McGiveney (*Court usher*), Francis Ravel (*French stage manager*), Adrienne d'Ambricourt (*Wardrobe woman*), Gil Stuart (*English photographer*), Cyril Delevanti (*Fanatic*), George Navarro (*Waiter*), Marcel de la Brosse (*Headwaiter*), Nestor Paiva (*Spanish peasant*), Alberto Morin (*Stage manager*), Maya van Horn (*Stout French woman*), George Davis (*Sleepy Frenchman*), Billy Griffith (*Pedestrian*), Geoffrey Steele, George Pelling (*English photographers*), Wilkie de Martel (*Porter*), Frank Arnold (*Taxi driver*), Louisa Triana (*Flamenco dancer*), George Dee (*Concierge*), Claire Dubrey (*Concierge's wife*), Geneviève Pasques (*Shopkeeper*), Lilyan Chauvin (*Dancer*), Gregor Momdjian (*Stage manager*).

Released in USA, October 1957; first shown in GB, November 1957. Running time, 114 min.
Distributor: M-G-M.

CUKOR: I don't consider myself a director of musicals, like Minnelli or Stanley Donen. There's something illogical about musicals: people open their mouths and start singing, all of a sudden. It has to be done with a certain amount of style, not realistic at all. Did you notice how carefully colour was used in *Les Girls*? Hoyningen-Huene and I decided to give each girl a colour to herself, that would colour each girl's sequence. Sometimes there was no colour at all, which whets your appetite for later. As in Montand's office in *Let's Make Love*, all browns and beige. Or the saloon in *Heller in Pink Tights*, vivid red walls. Of course, we had Gene Allen working with us, a very talented designer and now, sometimes, a writer.

The most beautiful decor I ever had for a picture was for *Lady L.* Lesley Blanch, the ex-wife of Romain Gary and a talented novelist – she wrote the novel 'The Nine Tiger Man' which I wanted to do – worked with us and with Orry-Kelly, who did the costumes. When the time came to start, I left the production. I couldn't stand the leading lady.

Wild is the Wind (1957)

Production Company	Joseph H. Hazen Productions
Producer	Hal B. Wallis
Associate Producer	Paul Nathan
Director	George Cukor

Second Unit Director	Arthur Rosson
Assistant Director	Mickey Moore
Script	Arnold Schulman. Based on a scenario by Vittorio Nino Novarese and the film *Furia* (1946) by Goffredo Alessandrini
Director of Photography	Charles Lang, Jr (VistaVision)
Second Unit Photography	Loyal Griggs
Special Photographic Effects	John P. Fulton
Process Photography	Farciot Edouart
Editor	Warren Low
Art Directors	Hal Pereira, Tambi Larsen
Set Decorators	Sam Comer, Arthur Krams
Music	Dimitri Tiomkin
Songs:	
'Wild is the Wind'	Sung by Johnny Mathis. Music: Dimitri Tiomkin. Lyrics: Ned Washington
'Scapricciatello'	Music: Fernando Albano
Sound	Gene Merritt, Winston Leverett

Anna Magnani (*Gioia*), Anthony Quinn (*Gino*), Anthony Franciosa (*Bene*), Dolores Hart (*Angie*), Joseph Calleia (*Alberto*), Lily Valenty (*Teresa*), James Flavin (*Wool Buyer*), Dick Ryan (*Priest*), Iphigenie Castiglione, Joseph Vitale, Ruth Lee, Frances Morris, Fern Berry, Ken Hooker, Max Power, Courtland Shepard, Robert R. Stephenson, Jeane Wood, Trude Wyler (*Party guests*).

Released in USA, December 1957; first shown in GB, February 1958. Running time, 114 min.
Distributor: Paramount.

CUKOR: I came to the project in a roundabout way. John Sturges, who was set to direct, replaced Fred Zinnemann in *The Old Man and the Sea* and I took over *Wild is the Wind*. . . . It's all very reminiscent of 'They Knew What They Wanted'. I was happy to work with Magnani and I think she gave a very unusual performance, not her usual fiery thing, but more subtle, toned down.

Heller in Pink Tights (1960)

Production Company	Paramount
Producer	Carlo Ponti
Associate Producer	Marcello Girosi
Director	George Cukor
Second Unit Director	Arthur Rosson
Script	Dudley Nichols, Walter Bernstein. Based on the novel *Heller With a Gun* by Louis L'Amour

Heller in Pink Tights: Sophia Loren

Director of Photography	Harold Lipstein
Second Unit Photography	Irwin Roberts
Process Photography	Farciot Edouard
Colour Process	Technicolor
Colour Consultant	Richard Mueller
Special Colour Consultants	George Hoyningen-Huene (theatre sequences), Warren Wade
Editor	Howard Smith
Art Director	Gene Allen
Special Effects	John P. Fulton
Costumes	Edith Head
Music	Daniele Amfitheatrof
Choreography	Val Raset
Sound	John Wilkerson, Winston Leverett

Sophia Loren (*Angela Rossini*), Anthony Quinn (*Tom Healy*), Margaret O'Brien (*Della Southby*), Steve Forrest (*Clint Mabry*), Eileen Heckart (*Mrs Lorna Hathaway*), Ramon Novarro (*DeLeon*), Edmund Lowe (*Manfred 'Doc' Montague*), George Mathews (*Sam Pierce*), Edward Binns (*Sheriff McClain*), Warren Wade (*Hodges*), Frank Silvera (*Santis*), Robert Palmer (*McAllister*), Cal Bolder (*Goober*), Leo V. Matranga, Taggart Casey (*Gunslingers*), Howard McNear (*Photographer*), Taylor 'Cactus' McPeters (*Williams*), Frank Cordell (*Theodore*), David Armstrong (*Achilles*), Alfred Tonkel (*Calchas*), Paul T. Salata, Robert Darin, John Rockwell (*Servants*), Bryn Davis (*Venus*), Cathy Cox (*Juno*), Riza Royce, Ruth Barnell, Allan Paige, Syl Lamont (*Peasants*), William Troy, William Vaughan (*Noblemen*), Geraldine Wall (*Madam*), Amanda Randolph (*Maid*), Richard Shannon (*Man at desk*), Harry Cheshire, Brad Johnson, John Benson, Bob Burrows, Jeffrey Sayre (*Poker players*), Bill Boyce, Charles Boaz, Paul J. McGuire, Ralph Neff, Harry J. Fleer, Neil K. Hooker (*Gamblers*), Dick Ryan (*Bartender*), Iron Eyes Cody, Eddie Little Sky, Rodd Reddwing, Chief Yowlachie (*Indians*), Kenneth D. Clark (*Western Union clerk*), Joe Forte (*Indian agent*), Dean Williams (*Kansas sheriff*), Gary Armstrong (*Office boy*), Bob Adler (*Stagecoach driver*), Lorraine Crawford (*Madam*).

Released in USA and GB, March 1960. Running time, 100 min.
Distributor: Paramount.

CUKOR: This was more or less inspired by Ada Menken, who toured the West with old plays like *Mazeppa* and *La Belle Hélène*. Not much of a plot, true, but a wonderful opportunity to recreate the West and the theatre of the period. It was very carefully reconstructed. Hoyningen-Huene went into the Paramount wardrobe department and rescued the old-fashioned costumes. And Sophia can really wear clothes. George [Hoyningen-Huene] was delighted with her; he took this very beautiful set of old tintypes.

Let's Make Love (1960)

Production Company	20th Century-Fox
Producer	Jerry Wald
Director	George Cukor
Assistant Director	David Hall
Script	Norman Krasna
Additional Material	Hal Kanter
Director of Photography	Daniel L. Fapp (CinemaScope)
Colour Process	DeLuxe
Colour Co-ordinator	Hoyningen-Huene
Editor	David Bretherton
Art Directors	Lyle R. Wheeler, Gene Allen
Set Decorators	Walter M. Scott, Fred M. Maclean
Credits and Opening Sequence Designer	Gene Allen
Music	Lionel Newman
Music Associate	Earle H. Hagen
Songs:	Sammy Cahn, James Van Heusen
'Incurably Romantic'	
'Specialization'	
'Hey You With the Crazy Eyes'	Sung by Frankie Vaughan
'The Pop Singer's Lament'	
'Lets Make Love'	Sung by Frankie Vaughan, Marilyn Monroe, Yves Montand
'My Heart Belongs to Daddy'	Cole Porter. Sung by Marilyn Monroe
Choreography	Jack Cole
Costumes	Dorothy Jeakins
Sound	W. D. Flick, Warren B. Delaplain

Marilyn Monroe (*Amanda Dell*), Yves Montand (*Jean-Marc Clement*), Tony Randall (*Alex Coffman*), Frankie Vaughan (*Tony Danton*), Wilfrid Hyde-White (*George Wales*), David Burns (*Oliver Burton*), Michael David (*Dave Kerry*), Mara Lynn (*Lily Niles*), Dennis King, Jr (*Abe Miller*), Joe Besser (*Charlie Lamont*), Madge Kennedy (*Miss Manners*), Ray Foster (*Jimmie*), Mike Mason (*Yale*), John Craven (*Comstock*), Harry Cheshire (*Minister*), Benny Burt (*Taxi driver*), Richard Collier (*Street sweeper*), Lennie Bremen (*Waiter at snack bar*), Gene Kelly, Bing Crosby, Milton Berle (*Themselves*).

Released in USA and GB, September 1960. Running time, 118 min.
Distributor: 20th Century-Fox.

CUKOR: Marilyn Monroe was a miraculous phenomenon of the screen. Her performance was done in very minute bits and yet, when you put them all together, they fitted together, perfectly smooth ... It was all very tragic. When we started

177

Something's Got to Give two years later, she couldn't remember her lines. She was so intelligent that she knew she was not good. But, somehow, you couldn't reach her any longer, she was like underwater. After seven weeks' work, we had only five days' worth. She finally was replaced by Lee Remick, but only for a short while. The picture was stopped and two months later Marilyn was dead.

Song Without End (1960)

Production Company	Columbia
Producer	William Goetz
Production Assistant	Milton Feldman
Director	Charles Vidor (and, uncredited, George Cukor)
Assistant Director	Carter DeHaven, Jr
Script	Oscar Millard
Director of Photography	James Wong Howe (CinemaScope)
Colour Process	Technicolor
Colour Consultant	Henry Jaffa
Editor	William A. Lyon
Art Director	Walter Holscher
Set Decorator	William Kiernan
Music	Selections from Liszt, Chopin, Wagner, Bach, Paganini, Handel, Beethoven, Mendelssohn, Verdi, Schumann
Music Adaptation	Harry Sukman
Musical Supervisor	Morris Stoloff
Music Consultant	Abram Chasins
Music Co-ordinator	Victor Aller
Vocal Ensemble	Roger Wagner Chorale
Piano Soloist	Jorge Bolet
Costumes	Jean Louis
Sound	Lambert Day
Music recording	Earl Mounce

Dirk Bogarde (*Franz Liszt*), Capucine (*Princess Caroline Sayn-Wittgenstein*), Geneviève Page (*Countess Marie d'Agoult*), Patricia Morison (*George Sand*), Ivan Desny (*Prince Nicholas*), Martita Hunt (*Grand Duchess of Weimar*), Lou Jacobi (*Potin*), Albert Rueprecht (*Prince Felix Lichnowsky*), Marcel Dalio (*Chelard*), Lyndon Brook (*Richard Wagner*), Walter Rilla (*Archbishop*), Hans Unterkirchner (*Czar*), E. Erlandsen (*Thalberg*), Alex Davion (*Frederic Chopin*), Katherine Squire (*Anna Liszt*), John Abbott.

Released in USA, October 1960; first shown in GB, September 1960. Running time, 145 min.
Distributor: Columbia.

CUKOR: Charles Vidor, a good friend of mine, was directing a picture about Franz Liszt in Austria called *The Magic Flame*. He died after three weeks of shooting and I took over for the producer. I didn't want to take credit for it, as it had been his project and not mine, but Goetz included a note of thanks in the credits.

The Chapman Report (1962)

Production Company	Darryl F. Zanuck Productions
Producer	Richard D. Zanuck
Director	George Cukor
Assistant Director	Serge Petchnikoff
Script	Wyatt Cooper, Don M. Mankiewicz, Arthur Sheekman. Based on the novel by Irving Wallace
Adaptation	Grant Stuart, Gene Allen
Director of Photography	Harold Lipstein
Colour Process	Technicolor
Colour Consultant	George Hoyningen-Huene
Editor	Robert Simpson
Production Designer	Gene Allen
Art Director	George James Hopkins
Music	Leonard Rosenman
Costumes	Orry-Kelly
Credits Sequence Designer	George Hoyningen-Huene
Sound	Stanley Jones

Efrem Zimbalist, Jr (*Paul Radford*), Shelley Winters (*Sarah Garnell*), Jane Fonda (*Kathleen Barclay*), Claire Bloom (*Naomi Shields*), Glynis Johns (*Teresa Harnish*), Ray Danton (*Fred Linden*), Andrew Duggan (*Dr George C. Chapman*), John Dehner (*Geoffrey Harnish*), Ty Hardin (*Ed Kraski*), Harold J. Stone (*Frank Garnell*), Corey Allen (*Wash Dillon*), Jennifer Howard (*Grace Waterton*), Cloris Leachman (*Miss Selby*), Henry Daniell (*Dr Jonas*), Hope Cameron (*Ruth*), Evan Thompson (*Cass Kelly*), Jack Cassidy (*Ted Dyson*), Roy Roberts (*Alan Roby*), John Baer (*Boy Barclay*), Chad Everett (*Water boy*), Alex Viespi (*Bardelli*), Jack Littlefield, Ray Foster (*Musicians*), Pamela Austin (*Teenage girl*), William Hummer (*Johnny Dillon*), Erma Amador, Elizabeth Camp, Blythe Daly, Beatrice Greenough, Riza Royce (*Club women*), Gloria Akin, Stuart Hall, Patricia Olson, Edith Tucker (*Guests*), Fern Barry (*Cook*), Michael Bell, Raymond Dannis, Pamela Grey, Peggie Leon, Terry Wayne, Yvonne White, Allen Zolezzi, Mikki Jamison, Zack Foster (*Little Theatre apprentices*), Fred Blau (*Teenage boy*), George Carey (*Grace's escort*), Roy Dean (*Drunk young man*), Jack Ellena, Norman Grabowski, Chuck Hicks, Steve Clinton (*Football players*), H. W. Gim (*Gardner*), Margo Loren (*Sarah's daughter*), Dorothy Love (*Mrs Simmonds*), Al Paige (*Butler*), Dean Plato (*Bartender*), Jack Richardson (*Man*), Ann Seaton (*Maid*), Malcolm Steen (*Man with Fred*), Grady Sutton (*Simon*), Geraldine Wall (*Receptionist*), Robin Warga (*Sarah's son*), Deborah Williams, Vicki Lee (*Suntanned kids*), Wendy Russell, Pat Marlowe, Dennis King, Jr, Mike Kostrick, Sam Colt (*Reporters*), Kenneth Jones

(*Photographer*), Lori Kaye (*Airline stewardess*), Charles Conrad (*Older married man*), Patsy Garrett (*Older married woman*).

Released in USA and GB, October 1962. Running time, 132 min.
Distributor: Warner Bros.

CUKOR: It was a casualty of *The Longest Day*. Zanuck was in Europe with *Day*, and *The Chapman Report* was recut before I knew what was happening. After the sneak preview in San Francisco, I told Richard [Zanuck] about some minor cuts that seemed necessary. The print and my suggestions were sent to Zanuck. Then, there was no time for discussion. The picture had to be released. The original version was well-balanced, it wasn't at all dirty, it was carefully planned to balance the most scabrous portions of the story with very delicate scenes, more intellectual. When the censors saw it, they demanded further cuts, of course.

When an audience laughs at the wrong moment, it doesn't mean that the scene at hand is wrong. It means that something that made that scene work has been removed. You build up to a certain pitch. Well, I believe there was not a scene in *The Chapman Report* that was not cut differently than the form originally planned. I'm not trying to claim it as a masterpiece or anything of the sort. But it had a certain dignity, especially in the episode concerning Claire Bloom, who was a tragic figure.

My Fair Lady (1964)

Production Company	Warner Bros.
Producer	Jack L. Warner
Director	George Cukor
Assistant Director	David Hall
Script	Alan Jay Lerner. Adapted from his book for the Broadway show based on George Bernard Shaw's *Pygmalion*
Director of Photography	Harry Stradling (SuperPanavision 70)
Colour Process	Technicolor
Editor	William Ziegler
Production Designer	Cecil Beaton
Art Director	Gene Allen
Set Decorator	George James Hopkins
Music	Frederick Loewe
Musical Director	André Previn
Orchestrations	Alexander Courage, Robert Franklyn, Al Woodbury
Vocal Arrangements	Robert Tucker
Songs	Frederick Loewe, Alan Jay Lerner
'Why Can't the English?'	Sung by Rex Harrison
'Wouldn't It be Loverly?'	Sung by Audrey Hepburn
'With a Little Bit of Luck'	Sung by Stanley Holloway
'I'm an Ordinary Man	Sung by Rex Harrison
'Just You Wait'	Sung by Audrey Hepburn

'The Rain in Spain'	Sung by Audrey Hepburn, Rex Harrison, Wilfrid Hyde-White
'Ascot Gavotte'	Sung by the chorus
'On the Street Where You Live'	Sung by Jeremy Brett
'I Could Have Danced All Night'	Sung by Audrey Hepburn
'You Did It'	Sung by Rex Harrison, Wilfrid Hyde-White
'Show Me'	Sung by Audrey Hepburn, Jeremy Brett
'Get Me to the Church on Time'	Sung by Stanley Holloway
'A Hymn to Him'	Sung by Rex Harrison, Wilfrid Hyde-White
'Without You'	Sung by Audrey Hepburn
'I've Grown Accustomed to Her Face'	Sung by Rex Harrison
Costumes	Cecil Beaton
Choreography	Hermes Pan
Sound	Francis J. Scheid, Murray Spivack

Audrey Hepburn (*Eliza Doolittle*), Rex Harrison (*Henry Higgins*), Stanley Holloway (*Alfred P. Doolittle*), Wilfrid Hyde-White (*Colonel Hugh Pickering*), Gladys Cooper (*Mrs Higgins*), Jeremy Brett (*Freddy Eynsford-Hill*), Theodore Bikel (*Zoltan Karpathy*), Isobel Elsom (*Mrs Eynsford-Hill*), Mona Washbourne (*Mrs Pearce*), John Alderton (*Jamie*), John McLiam (*Harry*), Ben Wrigley, Clive Halliday, Richard Peel, James O'Hara (*Costermongers*), Kendrick Huxham (*Elegant bystander*), Walter Burke (*Main bystander*), Queenie Leonard (*Cockney bystander*), Laurie Main (*Hoxton man*), Maurice Dallimore (*Selsey man*), Owen McGiveney (*Man at coffee stand*), Jack Raine (*Male member*), Raymond Foster, Joe Evans, Marie Busch, Mary Alexander (*Ad Lib Cockneys*), Marjorie Bennett (*4th Cockney*), Britannia Beatey (*Daughter of elegant bystander*), Beatrice Greenough (*Grand lady*), Hilda Plowright (*2nd bystander*), Dinah Anne Rogers (*1st maid*), Lois Battle (*2nd maid*), Jacqueline Squire (*Parlour maid*), Gwen Watts (*Cook*), Eugene Hoffman, Kai Farrelli (*Jugglers*), William Linkie, Henry Sweetman, Andrew Brown, Samuel Holmes, Thomas Dick, William Taylor, James Wood, Goldie Kleban, Elizabeth Aimers, Joy Tierney, Lenore Miller, Donna Day, Corinne Ross, Phyllis Kennedy, Dave Robel (*Ad Lib Cockneys*), Iris Bristol (*Flower girl*), Gigi Michel, Sandy Steffens, Sandy Edmundson, Merlene Marrow, Carol Merrill, Sue Bronson, Lea Genovese (*Ad Lib Toffs*), Frank Baker (*3rd elegant bystander*), Eric Heath (*5th Costermonger*), Jack Greening (*George*), Ron Whelan (*Algernon*), John Holland (*Butler*), Roy Dean (*Footman*), Charles Fredericks (*King*), Lily Kemble-Cooper (*Lady Ambassador*), Grady Sutton, Orville Sherman, Harvey Dunn, Barbara Morrison, Natalie Core, Helen Albrecht, Diana Bourbon (*Ad Libs at Ascot*), Moyna MacGill (*Lady Boxington*), Colin Campbell (*Man at Ascot*), Marjorie Hawtrey (*Ad Lib at Ascot*), Baroness Rothschild (*Queen of Transylvania*), Ben Wright (*Footman at the ball*), Oscar Beregi (*Greek Ambassador*), Betty Blythe (*Ad Lib at ball*), Buddy Bryan (*Prince*), Nick Navarro (*Dancer*), Tom Cound, William Beckley (*Footmen*), Paulle Clark, Allison Daniell (*Ad Libs at Ascot*), Alan Napier (*Ambassador*), Geoffrey Steele (*Taxi driver*), Jennifer Crier (*Mrs Higgins' maid*), Pat O'Moore (*1st *man*), Alma Lawton (*Flower girl*), Victor Rogers (*Policeman*), Michael St Clair (*Bartender*), Olive Reeves Smith (*Mrs Hopkins*), Brendon Dillon (*Leaning man*), Jennifer Raine (*Flower girl*), Ron Whelan (*Bartender*), Miriam Schiller (*Landlady*), Barbara Pepper, Ayllene Gibbons, Elzada Wilson, Jeanne Gerson, Buddy Shaw, Jack Goldie, Sid Marion, Stanley Fraser, George Pelling, Colin Kenny, Phyllis Kennedy, LaWana Backer, Monika Henried, Anne Dore, Pauline Drake, Shirley Melline, Wendy Russell, Meg Brown, Clyde Howdy, Nicholas Wolcuff, Martin Eric, John Mitchum (*Ad Libs at Pub in 'Get Me to the Church on Time' number*). Marnie Dixon sings for Audrey Hepburn.

Released in USA, October 1964; first shown in GB, January 1965. Running time, 170 min.
Distributor: Warner Bros.

CUKOR: I didn't try to tamper with *My Fair Lady*. It was perfect on stage. It had cinema effects, like dissolves. On the contrary, I tried to preserve the theatrical aspect of certain scenes, like the Ascot number. And the entire picture, of course, is highly stylized. It had to be, it's a musical. Gene Allen did the set design, leaving the costumes to Beaton, who's a specialist of the Edwardian era. The play was already based, not on the original Shaw, but on the picture made with Wendy Hiller and Leslie Howard. What I liked most about it was the fact that it was less of a romantic love story than a battle of wits.

Justine (1969)

Production Company	Berman-Century/20th Century-Fox
Producer	Pandro S. Berman
Associate Producer	Kathryn Hereford
Director	George Cukor
Production Managers	Saul Wurtzel, Joseph C. Behm
Assistant Director	Maurice Vaccarino
Script	Lawrence B. Marcus. Based on *The Alexandria Quartet* by Lawrence Durrell
Director of Photography	Leon Shamroy (Panavision)
Colour Process	DeLuxe
Special Photographic Effects	L. B. Abbott, Art Cruickshank
Editor	Rita Roland
Art Directors	Jack Martin Smith, William Creber
Set Decorators	Walter M. Scott, Raphael Bretton
Costumes	Irene Sharaff
Music	Jerry Goldsmith
Orchestrations	Arthur Morton
Choreography	Gemze de Lappe
Sound	Bernard Freericks, David Dockendorff
Technical Adviser	Dr Aaron Haddad

Anouk Aimée (*Justine*), Dirk Bogarde (*Pursewarden*), Robert Forster (*Narouz*), Anna Karina (*Melissa*), Philippe Noiret (*Pombal*), Michael York (*Darley*), John Vernon (*Nessim*), Jack Albertson (*Cohen*), Cliff Gorman (*Toto*), George Baker (*Mountolive*), Elaine Church (*Liza*), Michael Constantine (*Memlik Pasha*), Marcel Dalio (*French Consul General*), Michael Dunn (*Mnemjian*), Barry Morse (*Maskelyne*), Severn Darden (*Balthazar*), Amapola Del Vando (*Mrs Serapamoun*), Abraham Sofaer (*Proprietor*), Peter Mamakos (*Kawwass*), Stanley Waxman (*Serapamoun*), De Ann Mears (*Woman at ball*), Tutte Lemkow (*Prisoner*).

Released in USA, August 1969; first shown in GB, September 1969. Running time: 116 min.
Distributor: 20th Century-Fox.

CUKOR (1969): I can't have the greatest conviction about it, as I didn't prepare it. (*Justine* was started by Joseph Strick, who shot eight weeks on location in Tunisia. Ed.) There are several scenes in it I don't like at all. I also inherited the cast.

I also believe in working from the text, but not *that* slavishly. You must respect it, especially if it's a distinguished text like *Justine*. However, if you feel it's wrong, have it changed. Larry Marcus and I have gone back to the original. Durrell has something in the Prologue to *Justine* which is the key, I think. Let me read it to you: 'I am accustoming myself to the idea of regarding every sexual act as a process in which four people are involved. We shall have a lot to discuss about that.' It's from the letters of Sigmund Freud. It's like the story of someone's life, you have to find out what the principal element was. The same thing with the reflections of a love affair. One must try for the infinite complexity of the novel, however impossible.

For instance, the scene you saw being shot. In the café scene, the script is nothing but a description of events: three dancers and Melissa come out and she is inept. That's an intellectual concept: an inept dancer could be pathetic or comic. The story point is that she doesn't have her heart in it. She has the professional smile but to her it's all a routine she's bored with. You have to render all that with the business you create for the girl.

The three other girls dance very well, they look strange, big, so I made them wear face veils and since you never really see them next to the real girl, you cannot be sure what they are. I think the audience will catch on right then and there. It has to be subtle.

It should be a longish film, close to three hours, I'd say. (The version released ran under two hours. Ed.)

As far as my work is concerned, I'm excited about it every moment of the time. You've seen me make all those faces when I direct. I'm not aware of it. When you're a director, not only do you direct, you also react, you are the audience. The actors feel it. You must be a discriminating audience, a critical audience, so they will have the courage to try something different. On stage, if an actor does something stupid, the audience would boo him. But, if they do something right, the audience will catch it and encourage it. That's one part of the director's work. The other is the creative part: he is *more* than an audience, he also has to instruct, lead, really direct. Direct is the exact word for what you do.

A lot of people don't think that directing requires an awful lot of skill. I think it does, I think it's frightfully important. A man does one thing one week and the next he is a big director. The question is how long you can sustain it, how much do you know of your job. To undertake a production requires, in addition to everything else, experience, a certain amount of stamina and a certain amount of guts. You've got to be able to stand a great deal, to answer fifty questions they ask you every day, you have to make decisions right or wrong, immediately. I like it, I don't like it, it's too fast, it's too slow. And just plunge forward and trust yourself. Also, have the courage to do something that's wrong. And this comes only with experience.

The more successful you are as a director, a certain kind of director, the least apparent your hand should appear. There are directors who are wonderful, but they don't do it through the actors particularly. I happen to work through the actors.

Travels With My Aunt (1972)

Production Company	M-G-M
Producers	Robert Fryer, James Cresson
Associate Producer	Russell Thacher
Production Managers	Lloyd Anderson, Luis Roberts
Spanish Production Supervisor	Miguel Angel Gil Sr
Director	George Cukor
2nd Unit Director	John Box
Assistant Director	Miguel Angel Gil Jr
Script	Jay Presson Allen, Hugh Wheeler. Based on the novel by Graham Greene
Director of Photography	Douglas Slocombe (Panavision)
Colour Process	Metrocolor
Editor	John Bloom
Production Designer	John Box
Art Directors	Gil Parrondo, Robert W. Laing
Set Decorator	Dario Simoni
Music	Tony Hatch
Song: 'Serenade of Love'	Tony Hatch, Jackie Trent
Costumes	Anthony Powell
Titles	Wayne Fitzgerald, The Golds West
Sound	Derek Ball, Harry W. Tetrick

Maggie Smith (*Aunt Augusta*), Alec McCowen (*Henry Pulling*), Lou Gossett (*Wordsworth*), Robert Stephens (*Visconti*), Cindy Williams (*Tooley*), Robert Flemyng (*Crowder*), José Luis Lopez Vazquez (*Dambreuse*), Raymond Gérôme (*Mario*), Daniel Emilfork (*Hakim*), Corinne Marchand (*Louise*), John Hamill (*Crowder's Man*), David Swift (*Detective*), Bernard Holley (*Bobby*), Valerie White (*Mme Dambreuse*), Antonio Pica (*Elegant Man*), Alex Savage (*Minister*), Olive Behrendt (*Madame*), Nora Norman (*Stripper*), Aldo Sanbrell (*Hakim's assistant*), Charlie Bravo (*Policeman*), Cass Martin (*Skipper*), Javier Escriva (*Dancer*), Dennis Vaughan (*Minister in crematorium*), William Layton (*Art expert*), Julio Peña (*M. Alexandre*).

184

Released in USA, December 1972; first shown in GB, 15 February 1973. Running time, 109 min.
Distributor: M-G-M (US), MGM–EMI (GB).

Love Among the Ruins (1975)

Production Company	ABC Circle Films
Producer	Allan Davis
Production Supervisor	Herb Jellinek
Production Manager	John Palmer
Director	George Cukor
Assistant Director	Colin M. Brewer
Script	James Costigan
Director of Photography	Douglas Slocombe (in colour)
Editor	John F. Burnett
Art Director	Carmen Dillon
Assistant Art Directors	Tessa Davies, Brian Ackland-Snow
Music	John Barry
Lyrics	Don Black
Costumes	Margaret Furse
Titles	Dan Perri
Sound	John Bramall, Richard Portman, Bill Cook

Katharine Hepburn (*Jessica Medlicott*), Laurence Olivier (*Sir Arthur Granville-Jones, KC*), Colin Blakely (*J. F. Devine, KC*), Richard Pearson (*Druce*), Joan Sims (*Fanny Pratt*), Leigh Lawson (*Alfred Pratt*), Gwen Nelson (*Hermione Davis*), Robert Harris (*Judge*), Peter Reeves (*Malden*), John Blythe (*Tipstaff*), Arthur Hewlett (*Usher*), John Dunbar (*Clerk of the court*), Iain Sinclair (*Pratt's solicitor*), Mervyn Pascoe (*1st barrister*), Colin Thomas (*2nd barrister*), Lincoln Wright (*3rd barrister*), Edward Arthur (*4th barrister*), John Bromley (*5th barrister*), Leslie Southwick (*6th barrister*), Stanley Platts (*Foreman of the jury*), Philip Lennard (*1st reporter*), Peter Lund (*2nd reporter*), Frank Forsyth (*Jessop*), John Heller (Headwaiter), Rosamond Burne (*1st woman spectator*), Coral Fairweather (*2nd woman spectator*), Jacqueline Clarke (*Miss Pratt*), T. C. Hogan (*Teplow*).

First shown in USA on television (ABC), 6 March 1975; first shown in GB at London Film Festival, 4 December 1975.

The Bluebird (1976)

Production Company	Edward Lewis Productions (USA)/Lenfilm (USSR)
Executive Producer	Edward Lewis
Producer	Paul Maslansky, Alexander Archansky
Production Managers	Oleg Danilov, John Palmer, Teddy Joseph

185

Director	George Cukor
Script	Alexei Kapler, Hugh Whitmore. Based on the play by Maurice Maeterlinck
Directors of Photography	Jonas Gritsus, Freddie Young (in colour)
Editors	Tatiana Shapiro, Ernest Walter
Art Director	Valery Jurkevitch
Special Effects	Gregory Senotov, Alexander Zavialov, Roy Field
Music	Andrei Petrov
Lyrics	Julia Drunina, Tony Harrison
Musical Arranger	Irwin Kostal
Costumes	Marina Azizian, Edith Head
Sound	Gregory Elbert, Gordon Everett, John Bramall

Elizabeth Taylor (*Mother/Maternal Love/Witch/Light*), Nadia Pavlova (*The Bluebird*), Jane Fonda (*Night*), Ava Gardner (*Luxury*), Georgy Vitzin (*Sugar*), Cicely Tyson (*Cat*), Margarita Terekhova (*Milk*), Robert Morley (*Father Time*), Oleg Popov (*Fat Laughter*), Patsy Kensit (*Mytyl*), Todd Lookinland (*Tyltyl*), Will Geer (*Grandfather*), Mona Washbourne (*Grandmother*), Leonid Nevedomsky (*Father*), George Cole (*Dog*), Richard Pearson (*Bread*), Valentina Ganibalova (*Water*), Eugene Tscherbakov (*Fire*).

Distributor: 20th Century-Fox.

3. OTHER WORK

During the Second World War, Cukor made a US Army training film, *Resistance and Ohm's Law* in 1943 ('I had no idea what I was doing, had never heard of Ohm's Law').

In 1974, he was Executive Producer of *The Movies* (producer, Gary Essert), a two-part, four-hour history of the American film, produced in Hollywood for the benefit of the Motion Picture and Television Fund and co-ordinated by the Los Angeles International Film Exposition.

B. Uncredited Work

The Animal Kingdom (1932)

Production Company	RKO Radio
Directors	Edward H. Griffith; George Cukor (uncredited)
Script	Horace Jackson. Based on the play by Philip Barry
Director of Photography	Lucien Andriot

With Ann Harding, Leslie Howard, Myrna Loy, Neil Hamilton, William Gargan.

187

No More Ladies (1935)

Production Company	M-G-M
Producer	Irving Thalberg
Directors	Edward H. Griffith; George Cukor (uncredited)
Script	Donald Ogden Stewart, Horace Jackson. Based on the play by A. E. Thomas
Director of Photography	Oliver T. Marsh

With Joan Crawford, Robert Montgomery, Charlie Ruggles, Franchot Tone, Edna May Oliver.

Gone With the Wind (1939)

Production Company	M-G-M
Producer	David O. Selznick
Directors	Victor Fleming; George Cukor, Sam Wood (uncredited)
Script	Sidney Howard. Based on the novel by Margaret Mitchell
Director of Photography	Ernest Haller; Lee Garmes (uncredited)
Colour Process	Technicolor

With Vivien Leigh, Clark Gable, Hattie McDaniel, Leslie Howard, Olivia de Havilland.

CUKOR: As in *Copperfield*, I worked with Selznick in the pre-production for almost a year. We went south to look at locations. I worked with Cameron Menzies, who designed the picture, and I also tested scores of actresses for the Scarlett role: Frances Dee, Lana Turner, Susan Hayward, Paulette Goddard, not to mention many established stars. I may have favoured Katharine Hepburn before Vivien Leigh came to Hollywood. The picture was under way then. Atlanta was burning and still we had no Scarlett. Myron Selznick suggested to David that she did a screen test.

In a recent television programme (*The Selznick Era*, Ed) you saw some of the tests but you didn't see Vivien's. There were four scenes in each test. One of the scenes was the one between Scarlett and Ashley by the stile, late in the story. Some of the other actresses may have been better in the other scenes, but Vivien played this one with the greatest feeling. As a matter of fact, she didn't match this in the actual film. We ran her test at a Memorial Dinner a couple of years ago and everybody was moved to tears . . .

Vivien Leigh started work on the picture in the middle of January. Three weeks later, I was dismissed as director of the film (13 February 1939, Ed). In spite of this, I remained very good friends with Selznick till the end, which is more than you can say for Victor Fleming, who took over from me. I must say that Selznick got shaky about everybody: he changed Sidney Howard, he changed the cameraman. He probably got shaky about me. Or maybe Gable didn't think that I knew quite how to handle him, although we were very polite to each other. Or maybe that I would throw the picture to the woman, which is all nonsense, as there is no throwing anything to anybody – it's all in the text.

I think there are scenes that I could recognize as mine: the scene with the Negro maid, Melanie's baby. Not the opening scene, however. That was reshot later by Fleming or Sam Wood. But in any case the girls were following the original concept of their roles, which I had laid out. It's all been exaggerated by now. I may have advised Vivien later on. I know that she used to spend Sundays in my house. We remained great friends, although I never directed her again. Shortly before her death, I approached her to play the part of the mother in *The Right Honourable Gentleman*, a project I was to direct. It interested her, she would have been marvellous, but it didn't happen. It may still happen, however. John Osborne wrote a brilliant treatment, and Rex Harrison would be the leading man.

I'll Be Seeing You (1945)

Production Company	Selznick International
Executive Producer	David O. Selznick
Producer	Dore Schary
Directors	William Dieterle; George Cukor (uncredited)
Script	Marion Parsonnet. Based on a story by Charles Martin
Director of Photography	Tony Gaudio

With Ginger Rogers, Joseph Cotten, Shirley Temple, Spring Byington, Tom Tully.

Desire Me (1947)

Production Company	M-G-M
Producer	Arthur Hornblow Jr
Directors	George Cukor, Jack Conway (uncredited)
Script	Marguerite Roberts, Zoë Akins. Based on the novel *Karl and Anna* by Leonhard Frank, adapted by Casey Robinson
Director of Photography	Joseph Ruttenberg

With Greer Garson, Robert Mitchum, Richard Hart, Morris Ankrum.

Cukor's version, completed under the title *Sacred and Profane* in August 1946, was from a screenplay by Zoë Akins and Sonya Levien

Hot Spell (1958)

Production Company	Paramount
Producer	Hal B. Wallis

189

Directors	Daniel Mann; George Cukor (uncredited)
Script	James Poe. Based on the play *Next of Kin* by Lonnie Coleman
Director of Photography	Loyal Griggs

With Shirley Booth, Anthony Quinn, Shirley MacLaine, Earl Holliman.

C. Uncompleted Work

Something's Got to Give (1962)

Production Company	David Brown Productions
Producer	Harry Weinstein
Director	George Cukor
Script	Adapted from the screenplay *My Favorite Wife* (1940) by Bella and Samuel Spewack, from a story by Bella and Samuel Spewack and Leo McCarey
Director of Photography	Franz Planer (CinemaScope)
Colour Process	DeLuxe

With Marilyn Monroe, Dean Martin, Cyd Charisse, Tom Tryon, Phil Silvers.

Abandoned because of Marilyn Monroe's illness and death. Finally remade in 1963 as *Move Over Darling* (director, Michael Gordon), with Doris Day, James Garner, Polly Bergen, Thelma Ritter, Chuck Connors.

D. Projects

'There were a few things that I wanted to do that didn't happen.'

1933 *Living in a Big Way*. A re-teaming of Marie Dressler and Jean Harlow after the success of *Dinner at Eight*.
1935 *The Garden of Allah*. For David O. Selznick. With Joan Crawford.
1937 *The Life of Enrico Caruso*.
1938 *Pride and Prejudice*. From a screenplay by Aldous Huxley, based on the novel by Jane Austen. With Norma Shearer and Robert Donat.
1939 *Pride and Prejudice*. With Vivien Leigh and Laurence Olivier.
1945 *The Razor's Edge*. For Darryl F. Zanuck. Screenplay by Somerset Maugham from his own novel. Cast to include John Russell, Maureen O'Hara, Bonita Granville.
1954 *Love Me or Leave Me*. With Ava Gardner.
1956 *Cat on a Hot Tin Roof*. For producer Lawrence Weingarten.
1964 *Peter Pan*. With Audrey Hepburn.

Cukor on set (1971)

1965 *The Rector of Justin.* From the novel by Louis Auchinloss. With Spencer Tracy.
1966 *The Right Honourable Gentleman.* From the play by Michael Bradley-Dyne, adapted by John Osborne. With Rex Harrison.
1967 *The Nine Tiger Man.* Screenplay by Terence Rattigan from the novel by Lesley Blanch. With Audrey Hepburn, Elizabeth Taylor, Robert Shaw.
Casanova. With Rex Harrison.
The Spiritualist. From the book by Trevor H. Hall. Screenplay by Walter Reisch and Ellen M. Violett. With Katharine Hepburn.

Acknowledgments

A good many people contributed facts, suggestions, insights and stills to this book. Others made it possible for me to study the Cukor films in detail. I would like to express my gratitude to David Bradley, John Cocchi, Bernard Eisenschitz, William K. Everson, William C. Kenly III, John Kobal, Don Koll, Dion MacGregor, Adrienne Mancia, Howard Mandelbaum, Roger McNiven, Mary Meerson, Donald Ogden Stewart and Romano Tozzi. Thanks also to the Academy of Motion Picture Arts and Sciences in Hollywood, the British Film Institute in London, the Museum of Modern Art and the Lincoln Center for the Performing Arts in New York, and the Cinémathèque Française in Paris. And, very especially, to George Cukor, who generously opened his collection of screenplays and photographs to me, and gave for hours the pleasure of his company.

Stills by courtesy of ABC Television, Columbia, MGM–EMI, Paramount, RKO, 20th Century-Fox, Universal, Warner Bros., the Stills Library of the National Film Archive, London, and George Cukor.

This book is for Fred de Graaff.